Sin in Cultural Context

Sin in Cultural Context

Understanding the
Old Testament notion of 'sin'
among the Kongo people
of Brazzaville

Sabine Müri

regnum

First published 2021 by Regnum Books International

This book is an abridged version of an original thesis which can be found here: https://eprints.mdx.ac.uk/21638/

Regnum is an imprint of the Oxford Centre for Mission Studies

St. Philip and St. James Church
Woodstock Road, Oxford OX2 6HR, UK
www.regnumbooks.net

09 08 07 06 05 04 03 7 6 5 4 3 2 1

ISBN: 978-1-5064-9752-5
eBook ISBN: 978-1-5064-9753-2

Typeset in Candara by Words by Design.

Cover photo by Jean Philippe Delberghe on unsplash.com.

The publication of this volume is made possible through the financial assistance of Evangelische Mission Weltweit e.V.

Distributed by 1517 Media in the US, Canada, India, and Brazil

Dedication

I dedicate this thesis to my late mother, Lilly Müri-Merz, who instilled in me early in my life a love for God and who taught me the first steps of trusting him and seeking his guidance and assistance in all my human daily affairs.

Acknowledgements

Firstly, I would like to express my sincere gratitude to my supervisors, whose input and encouragement enabled me to make this thesis what it is: to Dr Keith Ferdinando for his guidance and support of my PhD studies and for his patience and continued advice; to Dr Thomas Harvey for his help and guidance in the process of the research; to Dr Harriet Mowat for her valuable input in the last stages before completion.

I am indebted to Dr Mamy Raharimanantsoa and Dr Serge Locko, who provided the opportunity to teach at the Faculté de théologie protestante de Brazzaville (FTPB) and to work with the class as the most important research focus group. I am deeply indebted to the participants in the focus groups and the interviewees who willingly gave of their time to talk with me about their culture and insights.

This dissertation would not have been possible without the continued financial support and patience of my donors throughout the many years of my research. I thankfully acknowledge the initial financial support by the SIL International Kenneth Pike Endowment Fund. My sincere thanks also goes to my employer, the Wycliffe Bible

Translators / SIL-Congo, who generously let me use working hours for conducting the field study in Brazzaville.

My gratitude extends to Patricia and Jonathan Brown, who proofread my work with great patience and care, and to Heinz Wunderli, who put my graphic ideas down to paper. A special thank you goes to Carmen Crouse, who first encouraged me to start doctoral studies.

Finally, I would like to thank my dear friend Ruth Julian for her continued encouragement, accompanying me in times of difficulty and illness that threatened to end my research prematurely, but also in times of joy and laughter.

Contents

Setting the Scene

Brazzaville, Congo. On the morning of Sunday 4 March 2012, the depot of the armoured division stationed in the Mpila district blew up in a series of explosions. In the neighbouring districts of Ouenzé and Talangaï, two of the most densely populated areas of the city and home of over 350,000 residents, thousands of people were killed and around 20,000 people lost their homes. The damage to property and infrastructure was extensive.

The explosions were a humanitarian disaster. When the first explosion happened I was standing at the window drinking coffee. My cell phone rang. It was a friend who wanted to know if I had heard 'this'. While we were still talking, four things happened simultaneously. I heard another much louder roar, the house I was in shook as if in an earthquake, I heard glass splintering, and my friend on the phone started to scream. I could only think of two things: that war had broken out again and that my friend's house and mine had been hit by a missile. Later, both beliefs turned out to be untrue. My strange initial reaction – I wandered around in the centre where I lived, carrying with me my computer and insect repellent, looking for a safe place to be – left me deeply troubled for weeks.

Two days after the explosions the class that I taught at Faculté de théologie protestante de Brazzaville (FTPB) started, and I asked my students whose families had been affected. There was no response at first. Then, one of the students raised his hand hesitantly. His timidity surprised me because I knew him as an outspoken and self-confident student.

Because of the severity of the explosions and the impact the incident had on the city I decided to confront my students the next day with the allegations I kept hearing on the streets: that the damaged districts were populated only by *nordistes,* people coming from the northern part of Congo. The *sudistes* were maintaining that the explosions were retaliation by fate or even God. Now the *nordistes* were repaid for their atrocities during the war. The way many Congolese in Brazzaville interpreted the explosions showed that the civil war had not been settled in their hearts and minds; old wounds of ethnic conflicts and the civil war of the 90s were reopened and showed their ugly face again.

Confronting my students with the people's talk was a risk; they came both from the north and the south. I was not sure if I would be able to control the reactions, but the hope of finding in the future church leaders sitting in my class a different attitude from that of Mr and Mrs Average was too strong to resist. Recounting in class the people's talk and asking what the students thought about it was the spark that lit the powder keg. The classroom erupted into a shrill and heated battle of words, fifteen students yelling at each other, and for a short moment I thought that the situation would get out of hand. I managed to calm down the students after a while, on the one hand content because my intuition the day before turned out to be true; on the other hand disappointed because my Christian students and future church leaders displayed the same shocking attitude I had observed in the streets.

As a calming measure I steered away from the personal dismay of all of us to the safer waters of the impersonal and asked about the response of the Church to such tragedies in general. It did not take long before we had put together a list of (theoretical) responsibilities of the Church. The Church should provide social and spiritual assistance, assume authority by leading people to Christ and by supporting the public powers, stand up against civil rioting, show solidarity, and remind itself that it should be salt and light in the world and play a prophetic role in society. Because I had the impression that many of the students' hearts remained 'cold', and because that attitude aroused anger and even greater disappointment in me, I challenged the students with the question of why the Church should do all the things we listed. 'God commanded it' I did not let pass for the right answer, and I finally wrested from them the reply 'because of love'.

When I asked why God let that all happen, there was stirring in the class again. And then one student exclaimed, 'Well, somebody must have sinned!' Such evil, he was certain, does not happen unless it is invited in by somebody's wrongdoing. Many of the people in the streets maintained that it happened because of the atrocities against the *sudistes* during the civil war. After the class session a *sudiste* student approached me with tears in her eyes and said that what I recounted was true and that '*dans les bars, c'est la fête chez nous!*'[1] The general hostile feelings and animosity of my students against

---

[1] '*In our bars people celebrate!*' In the thesis all quotations were in French with English in the footnotes, but hereafter in this book all quotations will be in English.

3

each other stirred up a mix of anger, fear, sadness and desperation in my heart. And in the next lesson the following day I did something I do not usually do in a classroom: I preached at my students, adapting from Luke 13:1–9.

> At that very time there were some students from Mansimou present who told Jesus about the Soldiers and the Northerners who had lived in the districts of Mpila and Ouenzé and who were killed by the explosions. Jesus asked them, "Do you think that because these Northerners were massacred in this way they were worse sinners than all other Congolese? No, I tell you; but unless you repent, you will all perish as they did. Or those 13,000 people who lost their homes – do you think that they were worse offenders than all the others living in Brazzaville? No, I tell you; but unless you repent, you will all perish just as they did."

While I was talking one half of the students were taking notes feverishly as if they did not want to miss a word. Because the majority of those students had previously shown a certain aversion to writing, it surprised me greatly. My words that morning seemed to be worth taking down; they seemed to hit home. The other half sat still as never before, listening attentively, hanging on my every word. When I registered the atmosphere in the room I almost lost concentration; it was gripping and I knew that the message from Luke 13 was needed. And it had to be delivered by an outsider.

Introduction

Using such an opening story is unusual in a piece of academic work, yet that episode in March 2012 was in a strange way the apex of the whole undertaking. I decided to express the experience by simply telling the actual story, because any other more abstract form to portray the intensity and power of the moment would fail. What follows is the presentation of the research as it was conducted previous to March 2012.

Background

While I was conducting the research in Brazzaville, the capital city of the Congo Republic, I worked for an institution that maintained a 'New Testament first' approach to Bible translation. Within the overarching paradigm that acknowledges the task of leading people to faith in Christ as one of the most important missionary commissions, the New Testament first approach makes sense. The priority of leading people to Christ is closely linked to the New Testament message of Jesus dying on the cross. This message begs the question as to why Jesus died on the cross. The shortest possible answer is, 'because of sin'. This answer seems to be satisfactory to many missionaries, which is why often the intelligibility of this message is not further questioned. It is at this point, however, that my questions start. What is 'sin' and how can I explain it? Thus, both the understanding of God and 'sin' will be major points of reflection in this book.

The understanding of 'sin' has a history in the Congo context. Missionaries of the early twentieth century complained that the notion of 'sin' was never understood by the Kongo people. For them, 'sin' had to do with certain prescribed actions that they have omitted to carry out, or certain prohibited actions that they have carried out, and thus they did not view 'sin' as inherent in humanity. Consequently, the two concepts seemed to be incompatible. Examination of the underlying philosophy of life in African societies demonstrates the gulf that opens up between West-European and sub-Saharan African perceptions of life. Mutual comprehension seems impossible. Listening to Kongo people talking about good and evil made me wonder whether early missionaries' reports about the incompatibility of their concept of 'sin' with the Kongo culture were accurate after all.

Later missionary work recognized the necessity of contextualization, of setting Christian beliefs and practices within the local context, seeking forms of theological expression rooted in local culture. Contextualization is finding ways to enable people to understand the significance of core issues of Christian belief. The notion of 'sin' is such a core issue. 'An inability to speak persuasively about sin adversely affects one's ability to speak plausibly about everything else.'[2] The

---

[2] Robert J. Priest, 2007. "Experience-near theologizing" in diverse human contexts. In: Craig Ott and Harold A. Netland, eds. *Globalizing Theology: Belief and Practice in an Era of World Christianity*. Nottingham: Apollos, pp. 180–195, p. 183.

missionaries had built on sand because they had not taken into account the worldview of the Kongo people, the needed philosophy and irreplaceable foundation of the spiritual development.

Thus, I formulated several questions:

1. What is the Kongo concept of 'wrongdoing'?
2. What does the Kongo discourse on wrongdoing look like?
3. What tensions arise in a contextualization project initiated by a Swiss researcher?

'Sin'

The two predominant metaphors used in the Old Testament for sin are those of 'defilement' and of a 'weight or burden'.

The New Testament speaks in a different idiom, describing 'sin' as a debt, and the most commonly occurring terms are found in the word groups related to the nouns *hamartia* (missing a mark, failure to achieve a standard), *adikia* (doing damage, legal wrongdoing, unrighteousness, injustice), *parabasis* (violation of the law, deviation, transgression), *paraptōma* (offence, failure) and – less common but most influential on considerable theological controversial debates on 'sin' throughout the last centuries – *opheilēma* (debt).

In the New Testament, Jesus starts his ministry with the call to repentance *(metanoeō*, to turn around or change one's mind; see Mark 1:15), a term suggesting that the people have 'turned away' from God.

The Apostle John also speaks of 'sin' in the singular (unlike the synoptics) and understands it as slavery (8:31–36) and spiritual

7

blindness (9:39–41). The author of the Epistle to the Hebrews deals with the topic of 'sin' in the context of sacrifice, interpreting the work of Christ as purification from 'sins' (1:3). He calls for a strict break with 'sin' that deceives, seduces and ensnares (Heb. 3:13; 11:25; 12:1).

The Apostle Paul speaks of 'sin' (*hamartia*) usually in the singular, describing it as a power, an active force in human beings. Acting like a person, 'sin' reigns (Rom. 5:20) and enslaves (6:6); it calls up for service (6:12) and pays wages (6:23); it inhabits human beings (7:17) and takes them captive (7:20). In Paul's terms, sin is a form of enslavement that disables will and judgement.

It is striking that the New Testament predominantly looks at 'sin' from a soteriological perspective and from the perspective of forgiveness. The evolution of the metaphor of 'sin' as a debt and the finding that the biblical notion of 'sin' is multi-faceted and diverse challenged me to delimit the scope. Because I considered the Old Testament understanding of 'sin' as fundamental, and because I repeatedly observed that the Kongo context holds many affinities with the Old Testament Hebrew culture, I decided to concentrate on the Old Testament description of 'sin'.

Congo and the Kongo People

I conducted my research among church-related Munukutuba speakers in the southern part of Congo. This area, together with the Lower Congo in the Democratic Republic of Congo (DRC), from present-day Kinshasa to the city of Matadi and the coastal area from Pointe-Noire down to Angola, is the contemporary area of the Kongo. That area was part of the ancient Kongo kingdom with its capital city São Salvador. At its maximum extent in the sixteenth and seventeenth centuries the Kongo kingdom covered a vast area from the Niari River in the north (Congo), including the later independent kingdom of Loango on the coast, to the Kwango River in the east (DRC) and to Luanda in the south on the Atlantic coast in contemporary Angola.

The borders of the present-day independent states in the Kongo area go back to the Berlin Conference in 1884/85, where African land was distributed among the European colonial powers. The whole region of the Lower Congo was divided among three colonial powers: France obtained the northern part, Portugal the southern part plus Cabinda, and the lower reaches of the Congo River up to Stanley Pool went to the 'Congo Independent State' under the control of the Belgian king, Leopold II. This division was exclusively based on political and economic interests irrespective of ethnic considerations.

The Kongo people, often referred to as 'Bakongo', are presumed to be a unified ethnic group of Bantu origin. However, the Kongo kingdom comprised many different ethno-linguistic groups and sub-groups that still exist today. The origin of the Kongo people is still a mystery with different explanations, depending on political and economic interests. The term 'Bakongo' itself was probably created by colonial administrators and Christian missionaries, perhaps by association with the ancient kingdom of Kongo. After its abolition in the new colonial environment, the Kongo kingdom became the Kongo 'tribe' that was both larger and less historically defined than the kingdom had been. Even though most of the Kongo identify themselves according to the various discrete ethno-linguistic sub-groups to which they belong, there is also an overall sense of Kongo identity that can be observed, which separates Kongo people from 'others'. This is reinforced by the widespread use of Munukutuba as lingua franca in all areas of the former Kongo kingdom.

9

Ancient Kongo Kingdom in the 16th – 17th Century

My research was conducted exclusively in the southern part of Congo. The relatively rich literature I found on the Kongo mainly concentrated on the area of the Lower Congo in DRC.

Besides French, the official language of the country, the Kongo living in the southern part of Congo have widely adopted Munukutuba as lingua franca and the churches throughout Congo have adopted a similar practice.

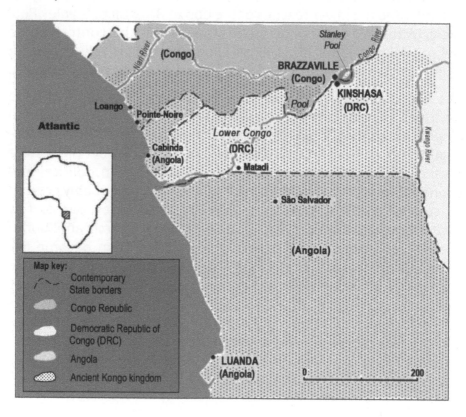

Culture and Worldview

Conducting research in Congo with Kongo people means working across cultures. For a long time, culture was an academic technical term describing an integrated form of human existence. This classic image produced a view of Africa as a patchwork of different 'cultures', each of which constitutes an integrated, bounded totality.

Closely related to culture is the concept of 'worldview'. It has its roots in Western philosophy, history and anthropology. Nineteenth-century historians were interested in looking at the structure of the world around them. Questions were asked about how cultural patterns emerged and spread or why some died out while others persisted for centuries or millennia.

The term 'worldview' has its limitations. Moreover, the world most people live in becomes increasingly fractured, influenced by postmodernity and globalization. Uniform worldviews hardly exist anymore. I still use of the concept of 'worldview', referring in this research to what the Kongo people take as given realities, their assumptions and values in their communities, the 'blueprint' or 'mental maps' they use to explain the nature of things, and that guide their behaviour.

Illustration of Worldview and Culture

In order to explain the term 'worldview' to the theology students with whom I worked, I adopted the image of the 'floating islands' (see figure overleaf). The illustration shows three levels of culture, in which worldview, as a part of culture, builds the foundational

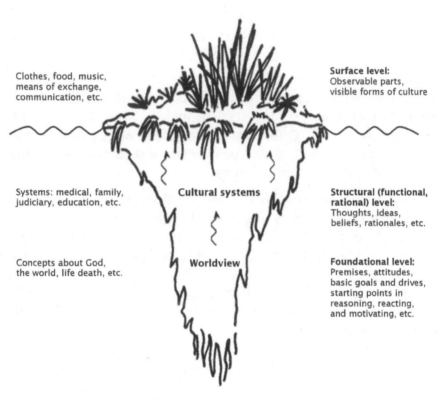

Clothes, food, music, means of exchange, communication, etc.

Surface level: Observable parts, visible forms of culture

Systems: medical, family, judiciary, education, etc.

Cultural systems

Structural (functional, rational) level: Thoughts, ideas, beliefs, rationales, etc.

Concepts about God, the world, life death, etc.

Worldview

Foundational level: Premises, attitudes, basic goals and drives, starting points in reasoning, reacting, and motivating, etc.

The 'floating island' of worldview

level,[3] where 'the underlying premises, emotionally charged attitudes, basic goals and drives, starting-points in reasoning, reacting and motivating' are found.[4] They are rarely questioned or reflected upon. Moving up a level, the structural level is reached, where the ideas are found that give reason and purpose for what will ultimately be acted out at the surface level. The latter is the observable part of culture that grows out of the structural level.

This view of worldview and culture is not uncontested but whatever concept is adopted, I think it is important to understand the categories through which reality is filtered. What I take as 'truth', the way I understand God, interpret biblical texts, or live the Christian faith, is influenced by my assumptions and preunderstandings deriving from my worldview. In this sense all theology is rooted in culture, which is the reason for using a qualitative research approach that allows me to tackle some of these assumptions and pre-understandings.

Scripture

The Old Testament and the New Testament form the biblical canon that I assume to be authoritative to the Christian church in the sense

---

[3] Justin Kimpalu, a Congolese investigator of culture who taught me the Munukutuba language, used the idea of floating islands to describe culture. Cultures are like the *Kongo ya sika* ('new Congo'), small islands of grass and weeds that can be observed floating on the water of the Congo River. What can be seen at the surface is only small compared to the root mass that is hidden from view yet holding the island together. The graphic realisation of the 'floating island' of worldview was done by me.

[4] Louis Luzbetak, 1988. *The Church and Cultures: New Perspectives in Missiological Anthropology.* Maryknoll, NY: Orbis Books, p. 78.

that it is a witness to and a 'vehicle' of God's authority. In the Bible God reveals himself, therefore I understand his Word as not communicating a 'thing' in the form of abstract sets of truths unrelated to space and time, fixed doctrines or dogmas, but communicating a person. The climax of God's self-revelation is found in Christ, the incarnate Word of God. Even though we 'have' God's word in written form, it must always be received anew in the various cultural settings and local situations, which is in a nutshell what contextualization is about.

Literature on 'Sin' in the African Context

African Christian theology refers to all African expressions of Christian faith in oral forms, symbols or writing by African Christian theologians using indigenous African thought, forms, concepts and worldviews. Publications dedicated to the notion of 'sin' in the African context are scarce and often buried under headings of 'fetishism', 'sorcery', 'witchcraft', exorcism, healing or salvation.

Sebahire Mbonyinkebe characterizes the African understanding of 'sin' as based on a sacred order and oriented towards the community.[5] What improves the life in a community is described as 'good'; anything contrary to it is called 'evil'. In Mbonyinkebe's catalogue of serious transgressions in African societies, 'sorcery' takes the first position. It is generally understood as a crime against life.

While many scholars claimed either that the Africans had no notion

---

[5] Sebahire Mbonyinkebe, 1974. 'Brèves réflexions sur la conception traditionnelle du péché en Afrique Centrale'. *Cahiers des religions africaines*, 8 (16), pp. 155-165.

of 'sin' or that they had a very poor concept of it, others claimed that African people not only know about 'sin' but, by breaking the sacred law respected by the community, they understand also a divine power being offended. This implies the belief that moral values are based upon the recognition of the divine will and that 'sin' in the community must be expelled if perfect peace is to be enjoyed. But despite some important and relevant insights into the notion of 'sin' in the African traditional religion, there is no specific work on it in the Kongo culture. The Christian community needs to be able to speak plausibly about 'sin'. The present study fills a considerable gap not only in the literature but also in the shaping and transforming of the local theological understanding of central issues of the Christian faith, which includes the Kongo people and me as the researcher alike.

Research Procedures

Various research methods were used in this study: working with different participation groups and conducting semi-structured interviews and exegetical exercises of various Old Testament texts. The different perspectives contributed to obtaining a deeper and clearer understanding of 'sin' and wrongdoing in the Kongo culture on the one hand, and a better understanding of the biblical notion of 'sin' on the other hand, using the four-step-model of 'critical contextualization' developed by Paul Hiebert,[6] and encapsulated in the figure overleaf.

---

[6] Paul G. Hiebert, 1987. 'Critical contextualization'. *International Bulletin of Missionary Research*, 11 (3), pp. 104-112. See also Hiebert, 1994. *Anthropological Reflections on Missiological Issues*. Grand Rapids, MI: Baker Books. The diagram of the model was developed by me during the research.

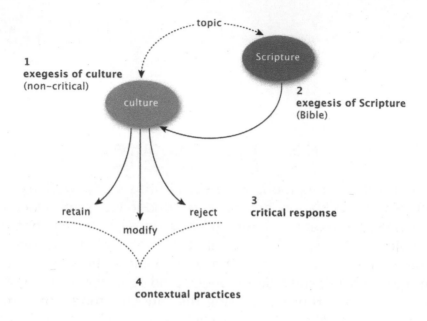

Four-step-model of critical contextualization

Exegesis of Culture –
The Kongo Understanding of 'Wrongdoing'

When I first began field study in Brazzaville I thought that the word 'sin' was too heavily loaded with biblical and West-European Christian theological teaching, and it was Loba who suggested that any intercultural exegesis in Africa needed to be measured against the African worldview that values the promotion of life.[7] Adopting Loba's suggestion I organized the first few questions in the participation groups around 'life', its promotion, its protection and destruction. Each participation group was asked to describe what *luzingu ya mbote* (good life) and what *luzingu ya yimbi* (bad life) meant to them.

Understanding Community

Material wealth

As a start, the catechumens, the first of three participation groups, described going to school or working as something good. This was followed by *'having financial capability'* and being rich, having a

[7] Jean-Claude Loba-Mkole, 2005. *Triple Heritage: Gospels in Intercultural Mediations.* Kinshasa: Centre de Recherches Interdisciplinaires de Limete; Pretoria: Sapientia Publishers.

businessman or merchant with a proper métier in the family. The young people in the city characterize the good life by material wealth, which means having a house, a car, conveniences, lots of money, moving in the best circles. If you do not have all these things you are considered an inferior person. Most people *'cling to the supporting pillar of the family'*, to the one who has money and resources. This is also applicable to the people living in the village, where the more traditional view of good life is different. In the village, good life means to have fields to till, harmony – knowing one's place and being useful – five wives, food, livestock and servants.

Harmony

The odd word in the list was 'harmony', expressed by *kintwadi* (agreement, [tacit] understanding, togetherness, being unified, association) and by *luzolo nsalasani* (mutual love/support). Harmony is demonstrated in greeting people and it is considered rude not to greet each other even if you already greeted the same person earlier. The simplest greeting *mbote mama* ('good morning' – addressing a woman) has more meaning than just being polite. To greet each other is a sign of *kintwadi*. *'It comforts us in our misfortune and joy'*. It is reassuring to know that the greeting person is on one's side sympathizing with one's situation. Not greeting is a serious matter and is perceived as evil.

> *If you don't say good morning, for us, it is really, it is a disaster ... He is the one who never greets others ... that already tells you that he is evil. He is not a good man, that one. He never says hello.*

Harmony is also shown to be important at other occasions of joy and grief: the birth of a child, a wedding, illness and death.

> Where we live, when someone died in the area, and you never show up, that's bad. You come and sit down for one hour, even if you don't give much [money or present], your presence is important.

Visiting the concerned person, sitting down for a short time, shows support; not visiting the concerned person is 'bad', evil.

Another element of that harmony is to know one's place in the community. One of the young men explained the model of *mbongi*, a traditional *paillotte* or straw gazebo, where the elders of a village meet in order to eat together and sort out community problems. Younger men are allowed to sit in these gatherings as well, on the condition that they don't speak up but listen to the elders and learn from them. It is equivalent to showing *buzitu* (respect), one of the cornerstones of the Kongo concept of community.

Community

Another element of 'good life' is (*di*)*kanda* (family/clan) and having a family is seen as a social obligation. Giving birth to at least one child is essential. As a woman '*without a child you are excluded; you are not respected*'. A 'bad life' was expressed as 'witchcraft', suffering, sickness, not having children, not being married, not being respected, not being successful and not having means, money or work.

In the Kongo, because life is sacred and family is THE most important thing in life, everything that supports or brings harmony to the family *is a must*.

Being married and having as many children as possible are more important than all the material richness one can get. Traditionally, polygamy is encouraged; monogamy is considered unsteady, like standing on only one leg. Not being married and not having children is as if one is dead, for nobody will carry on his name and the existence of the clan will end. The unmarried person is not 'considered' in the community. Everything is undertaken to remedy this serious anomaly that renders the childless person isolated.

In more general terms the community is understood as being the centre of life. 'Outside of the community the individual would be nothing more than a pitiable castaway'.[8] Balandier accounts for an old Kongo proverb saying that a Kongo person who has left his clan is like 'a grasshopper that lost its wings'.[9] By leaving his clan that person has crossed the borders outside of which security, solidarity and affection are no longer guaranteed. 'When the community is, I am; when it is not, I am not.'[10] In other words, I am because the community is; without it my existence becomes dull and meaningless. Family and community, with all their positive and negative obligations, lie at the very heart of the Kongo worldview. Thus, the key for a cultural outsider to understand wrongdoing and 'sin' in the Kongo culture lies within the conceptual framework of the family and community. A Christian-African ethic must not lose sight of African attitudes about life and community.

---

[8] Bernard Bakana Kolélas, 2006. *Le déchirement : roman*. Abidjan: CEDA/NEI, p. 134.

[9] Georges Balandier, 1965. *La vie quotidienne au royaume de Kongo du XVIe au XVIIIe siècle*. Paris: Librairie Hachette, p. 178.

[10] Simon Bockie, 1993. *Death and the Invisible Powers: The World of Kongo Belief*. Bloomington, IN: Indiana University Press, p. 10.

Insights from Exegetical Work of Biblical Texts

For self-critical reflections on the role of the community, 'sin' and wrongdoing, the second participation group, a group of theology students, worked on three Old Testament passages: Exodus 32:1–29 (The Golden Calf), Joshua 7:1–26 (Achan's theft and punishment), and 2 Samuel 11:1–12:14 (King David's adultery).

The individual is called to account

Working through the texts, the theology students expressed their bewilderment and incomprehension of Moses in Exodus 32, who orders 3,000 men to be killed after worshipping the golden calf that Aaron built, without finding out who the real culprits were. The students found it striking that Achan's 'sin' in Joshua 7 is attributed to all Israel and has consequences for a whole nation. It was moreover not understood why an individual person causes the punishment, condemnation and destruction of a whole family considered innocent [by the students]. It was incomprehensible to the students why the whole people were condemned although the covenant was violated by Achan only. Along the same lines, it was questioned why in 2 Samuel 11–12 the innocent child of David's adultery gets punished instead of him.

These things caused bewilderment because in Kongo culture, in case of a violation of a principle or law, it is not the family or community that is sanctioned, but the one who did wrong. The family is nevertheless affected and offended and there are consequences for the whole community because there is humiliation for the whole family, but the children are not punished for their parents' or brothers' fault. The culprit is not rejected but the clan invests in getting him out of the situation which he has brought on himself. Moreover, the family/community cannot be asked to put to death a brother, a parent or another clan. The death penalty is, however, given in the event that the prohibited is violated, especially when the sacred is profaned.

In many aspects the Kongo people are not different from other cultures when it comes to breaking norms of the community. One is punished, depending on the seriousness of the offence, if one does not respect the norms of the village, the clan, the family, or if the traditional laws are not observed. The Kongo bring charges in the case of offences such as stealing, lying, hiding, committing despicable acts, envying, committing adultery, that break the good relationship between the offended and the offender; also infidelity in a covenant between people, disrespect of agreed clauses, envy and greed.

*The chief is regarded as being responsible
for the wellbeing of the community*

What opened up the field a bit further was the students' comments on the leaders in Exodus 32 (Moses, Aaron, Levites) and 2 Samuel 11 (David).

One student expressed her incomprehension of the Levites who betrayed their brothers by taking sides with Moses in Exodus 32. Why did they not stay unanimously with the people saying, 'we live together, we die together'? It was also incomprehensible why Aaron remained unpunished. For another student it was bewildering that Aaron, God's servant, let himself be influenced by the perverse ideas of the people. If a chief let himself be led away as Aaron did, he would be condemned.

It was also incomprehensible why David committed adultery, and how he let himself be seduced so rapidly and violently, just to sleep with a woman without thinking of his honour. It is very rare that a village chief, a responsible person of high rank, would commit such a dishonouring act as David's adultery because, if the community is to prosper, the chief is obligated to behave well, to preserve his dignity and be a good example.

The centrality of the community

The students were very protective of the community and most Congolese suffer under the many exigencies imposed by the family and the clan; for example, providing shelter, food, money and gifts to those lacking in these things. These established traditional obligations are often experienced as burdensome and constraining and are linked with the constant fear of measures taken against them, such as curses that bring about sickness, misfortune, or accidents resulting from *kindoki* in the case of not meeting those obligations. The demands are increasingly seen as intolerable intrusions into the household economy. Non-compliance with family obligations festers under the surface or bursts into open conflict, calling on 'witchcraft practices' and having a serious impact on the perception of disease and even the mental health of the parties involved. *'The family is never satisfied. If you don't take care of her [the family], you become the victim of many troubles.'*

The centrality of community in African thought is firmly established in the extensive literature on the topic. It is community that shapes the understanding of the person as individual. Community and individual are intrinsically linked. Thus, researching into the understanding of community in the African context is at the same time researching into the understanding of the individual person. The community does not only consist of the men and women currently alive, but also of the departed ancestors whom Mbiti called the 'living dead', and the yet unborn.

One of the most famous quotes regarding the general understanding of community and its individual members in the sub-Saharan African context originates from Mbiti: 'I am, because we are; and since we are, therefore I am.'[11]

In other words, 'when the community is, I am, and when it is not, I am not'; an individual who is disconnected from the community is nothing. However, it is a misunderstanding to conclude from all this that the individual is self-less, but 'the communal world takes precedence over the individual life histories.'[12] Consequently one's moral obligations and rights in the African traditional view are based in and tied to the community. The community is life. And if one wanted to put forward any philosophical proof of human existence it would most certainly be close to Pobee's dictum: *cognatus ergo sum* – I am related, therefore I am.[13]

The identity of an individual member is given through *kanda*, the community. Outside of *kanda* there is no real existence. The *kanda* is the essential unit for the social structure; it is the framework within

---

[11] John S. Mbiti, 1990. *African Religions and Philosophy.* 2nd rev. and enl. ed. London: Heinemann, p. 106.

[12] Ifeanyi A. Menkiti, 1984. 'Person and community in African traditional thought.' In: Richard A. Wright, ed. *African Philosophy: An Introduction.* Lanham, MD: University Press of America, pp. 171–181, p. 171.

[13] John S. Pobee, 1979. *Towards an African Theology.* Nashville: Parthenon Press, p. 49.

which the perception of the world is forged. Members of the *kanda* community are the living, the *bakulu* (the dead) and the children still to be born. The community bears responsibility for the individual member in such a way that an older brother, for example, can be made answerable for an offence committed by a younger sibling. A Kikongo proverb says: *Ngazi kudya banswini, lemina kubaka bantyetye* – the sparrows eat the nuts, but it is the larks that get thirsty. Interpreted to mean that when a child does a bad thing, it is its father who gets punished. This contradicts what the students said: that the real culprit must be found in order to settle the matter. Yet, when it comes to children who break the law, the situation might be judged differently. It is, however, undisputed that the action of a single person concerns the whole community because the individual is part of a greater whole. In order to be a powerful community, every individual member is expected to contribute, expressed in the phrase: *Mbu wazadiswa kwa zinzadi ye zinto* – the sea is filled by streams and rivers. And the strength and power of an individual lies in a strong community, as implied by the Kikongo proverb: *Ngolo za ngandu mu maza* – the strength of the crocodile is in the water. 'The individual who lacks the directives of the group is a deviant.'[14] *Nto wayenda yandikaka wayenda tengama* – the river meanders because it travels alone. The individual does not know how to behave on his own; going it alone is 'sickness' and leads to evil.

The community into which a Kongo person is integrated is illustrated overleaf. An individual's *kanda* represents the influence of the mother's side (matriline) which, in the past, and still to a large extent today, is the source of social power.

---

[14] Kajsa Ekholm Friedman, 1991. *Catastrophe and Creation: The Transformation of an African Culture.* Chur: Harwood Academic Publishers, p. 108.

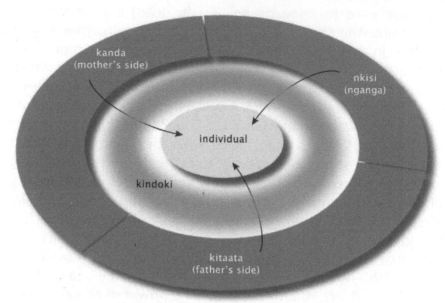

kanda
(mother's side)

nkisi
(nganga)

individual

kindoki

kitaata
(father's side)

Sources of influence and power

The mother's brother, the maternal uncle, also plays a significant role, giving not only material support, but also supernatural support. He protects and enables his nieces and nephews to develop through special power. When angered he might withdraw his protection with disastrous consequences, leading among other things to attacks by *bandoki* ('witches') who 'eat' the person, which results in the sickness or death of the 'eaten-up' person.

Kitaata represents the power of the paternal side of the family. Although the father and his *kanda* are given only secondary consideration, the father nevertheless occupies a special position and carries special obligations. He is entitled to scold, punish, assist or advise. The father has the right (*kitaata*) to receive gifts from his children (for example, part of the entrails of a shot animal, an occasional calabash of palm wine, the first catch of game, a prepared meal). When honoured, given respect in this way, he can bless a child. Blessing for a daughter means the ability to have children. Blessing for a son means having luck in his job and in making money. The father's curses are greatly feared. *Kitaata* is not only held by the father but also by the head of the family group, and the head of the clan has also the power to lock up, to bind, to render powerless and to curse, by which livestock and palm trees, for example, might also get affected. The father keeps his power even after death and is satisfied by offerings or sacrifice of different kinds.

The third sphere of influence and power is that of *nganga* and *nkisi*. *Nganga* is a traditional healer and a specialist in making *nkisi* objects ('fetishes') and operating them. *Nkisi* includes the idea of the medicine which the *nganga* uses but is also the abode for a protecting ancestor, the place where supernatural power is concentrated and an object through which one enters into contact with this power.

Kindoki is a fourth element exercising power and influence in the Kongo community system. Usually translated as 'witchcraft', it is closely linked with antisocial behaviour. The ones using *kindoki*-power, the *bandoki* ('witches'), are 'morose, unsociable people, people who eat alone and do not share, arrogant, passing by others without greeting, people who are readily offended'.[15]

---

[15] Laurenti Magesa, 1998. *African Religion: The Moral Traditions of Abundant Life.* Maryknoll, NY: Orbis Books, p. 170, quoting Lucy Mair, 1969. *Witchcraft.* New York: World University Library, p. 43.

Because of the communal outlook of the Kongo people, personal profit or any sign of antisocial activity falls under suspicion of *kindoki,* 'simply because doing better than your neighbour is what witchcraft is all about – they are the same thing'.[16] *Kindoki* 'manifests itself very strongly in connection with malice and theft'.[17] For somebody to be exceptionally blessed indicates that he/she has made use of *kindoki* to the disadvantage of someone else. Thus, if one wants to be successful, one must be careful to be generous in fulfilling one's obligations, otherwise one is suspected of having used witchcraft to attain one's position, since it is from jealousy and enmity that *kindoki* is born.

Abnormalities, such as infertility, sickness, an epidemic, an accident, famine or inexplicable death, are often seen as an indicator of the influence of *kindoki*. Chiefs, as the defenders of the public good, are empowered by *kindoki* in order to protect and defend against evil powers and curses. 'The witchcraft business is the Mother of all evil, the Grandmother of confusion, the Child of harm and the Grandchild of jealousy'.[18] *Kindoki* is 'the power of death and destruction'.[19]

'Witchcraft' (*kindoki*) is not to be understood as something of past 'uncivilized' or 'savage' ages, but it is 'intrinsic to the modern world'.[20] In daily life, however, *kindoki* is perceived as evil through

---

[16] Wyatt MacGaffey, 2000. *Kongo Political Culture: The Conceptual Challenge of the Particular.* Bloomington, IN: Indiana University Press, p. 34.

[17] A statement resulting from the third group (women's bible study group).

[18] John M. Janzen and Wyatt MacGaffey, 1974. *An Anthology of Kongo Religion: Primary Texts from Lower Zaïre.* Lawrence, KS: University of Kansas Publications. (Publications in Anthropology; 5), p. 48.

[19] Joseph van Wing, 1938. *Études bakongo II: religion et magie.* Bruxelles: Institut Royal Colonial Belge. (Mémoires, Collection in-8°; Tome IX, fascicule 1), p. 112.

[20] Wyatt MacGaffey, 2000. *Kongo Political Culture: The Conceptual Challenge of the Particular.* Bloomington, IN: Indiana University Press, p. 2.

and through. Because of his magical power to unmask *bandoki* and to identify the reasons for aggression in the family, the *nganga* is still often a sought-after and important person.

The above findings regarding the community and the insights on *kindoki* suggest that misfortune, sickness and death are forms of outside evil overpowering the individual. It would appear that explanations for wellbeing and success are to be sought outside of the individual as well. In such a worldview where everything depends on manipulating powers and having access to the external sources of such, the idea of a relationship with God – the perspective displayed in the biblical Scriptures – seems out of place. And thus the concept of 'sin' being a loss of or the break in the relationship with God is foreign to the traditional Kongo understanding of wrongdoing.

Understanding Theft, Disrespect and Broken Harmony

While harmony in the community and respect for elders, parents and older siblings were good things on the students' list, two bad topics stood out: firstly, theft, and secondly, everything that undermines 'family' or clan, such as not being married, not having children, or adultery.

Theft is never just a private offence for it is also disrespectful of parents and dishonours the whole family. It can also have severe consequences for the next generations. The students' comments were:

- Theft is '*yimbi (evil). There is no dignity in such practice.*'
- Theft '*leads to death and brings about sickness above all in cases of retaliation coming from fetishist practices.*'

- Theft *'encourages idleness and laziness and forces to lie and it leads to killing.'*

In the exegetical work done by the students, they expressed their incomprehension that Achan's theft in Joshua 7 was attributed to the whole of Israel and that the whole family had to submit to the punishment. In the Kongo culture the punishment of a thief is not inflicted on the family, although theft still affects the whole family. The students expressed in unison that the death penalty for Achan was unreasonable and the massacre of his (apparently innocent) family a sheer act of brutality. It was argued that it is important to lead the culprit to repentance and to integrate him into the community. Moreover, it is essential to know the culprit's motivation of his action before any punishment is imposed, and:

> Instead of killing [the wrongdoer], he is to be put into prison, followed by a systematic teaching (education) regarding the change of mentality in order to offer him the chance to affirm his good reputation in the tribe and in the family and why not also in the society.

Education of course can have different forms. Stories, tales, proverbs, but also the institution of *mbongi* as a place where the elders teach and educate the younger ones.

The students explained that the Kongo culture knows different traditional methods for divination to identify a thief. Palm oil is heated up until it is boiling; the suspect puts his hand into the oil; if he is not burnt, he is innocent. Alternatively, a fire is lit and the same procedure applied. Poison can serve as divination method as well. The suspect is forced to drink a poisonous drink; if he vomits the liquid, he is innocent. Another way is the application of *nkisi* (objects with concentrated supernatural powers), which then expose the culprit.

The punishment for theft is often a fine. But a notorious malefactor who continuously dishonours the family can be traded with salt, rice, animals, food or guns, and be sold far away as a slave. A person sold is called *mwana ntsumba* (bought child). To sell a culprit is to avoid killing him, although another method of punishment is to throw the

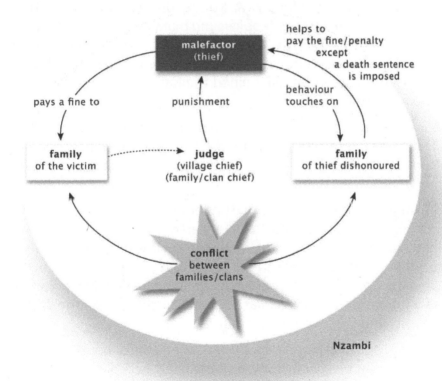

The dynamics of theft

wrongdoer alive into a deep hole and leave him to die. When he is dead, the hole is filled up and a baobab tree is planted on top as a symbol. Selling the culprit or allowing him to die are extreme measures taken only in intractable cases. The descriptions seemed strikingly close to the Joseph story in Genesis 37, which I pointed out to the students.

When a theft is discovered the head of the family usually takes care of the incident. In any other case, the village chief is appealed to. Often the high fine imposed on the culprit in a lawsuit cannot be paid without help from the family. A Kongo proverb describes that situation: *Kisa kya mante kyatebokela mu muntu muntu* – a cooking-pot is filled with spittle by one person after another. That kind of support of an offender, however, does not mean approval of their actions. As the wrongdoer has ruined the family's honour, justice is relentlessly carried out.

Because the thief is not an independent unit but an integral part of the family, his wrongdoing dishonours the family. Whatever the punishment, it is the thief's family's highest interest to gain back their honour.

To conclude that the Kongo people understand evil and wrongdoing as existing exclusively outside of a person, however, would be misleading. The human person, including their ethical living, needs to be understood holistically, in the sense that there is no separation between being and doing. There is no genuine healing in traditional Africa without rites of reconciliation, which include both the visible community and the invisible community.

In general, African ethics locates the seat of ethical conduct in the organs of the human person of which the heart occupies the primary position. The Munukutuba-word *ntima* (heart) is used in many different expressions. The heart is the seat of the human emotions and thoughts, of wisdom, of remembering and forgetting, of envy and desire, of good or bad character, of opinion and decision, perseverance, determination and indifference, but also of endurance and stamina. Somebody with *ntima ya kulemba* (tired heart) feels discouraged and depressed. *Ntima ya yimbi* (evil heart) stands for a bad character, lack of love and egoism; *ntima ya mbote* (good heart) stands for a good character and a kind personality. A liar, somebody being double-tongued or double-crossing another person is said to be 'double-hearted' – *kuvwanda na bantima zole* (to be with two hearts).

According to Bantu ethics the heart constitutes a serious limitation of the offender's responsibility; in fact, it yields to the culprit the position of a victim, exemplarily expressed by the rendering 'my heart has deceived me'. '"I" am never alone responsible for the "evil": the inhospitality of the cosmos, the malice of other humans and my "heart" are always accomplices.' [21] The 'heart' summarizes the external complicity of all sorts (lack of knowledge, physical weakness, etc.) and waters down the individual's responsibility to the point where it is reduced to nothing.

The differentiation between guilt- and shame-oriented cultures is an issue that is often raised in missiology. In this connection guilt and shame are understood as the two main reactions of conscience to violating norms. The violation of norms is viewed as wrong the moment it happens and not only when the violation is found out or 'seen' by the 'significant others'. It would appear, however, that the main reaction of the conscience of the Kongo people is found in the

---

[21] Ntumba Tshiamalenga, 1974. 'La philosophie de la faute dans la tradition Luba'. *Cahiers des religions africaines*, 8 (16), pp. 167-186, p. 183f.

area of fear, that is, fear of the consequences in any form of harm or evil. The fear of being found out and getting punished or falling ill is pervasive.

In summary: disrespect and theft interrupt the harmony in the community. The protection of the family is breached and invites attacks by *ndoki* (specialists practicing *kindoki*). Because family means life, and because *kindoki* is seen as the very enemy of life, *kindoki* is found very close to everything that threatens the unity and harmony of the family. In Kongo culture respect is an obligation. Respect for the senior person is of paramount importance. When there is a lack of respect it is difficult for the individual to be forgiven.

It is important to note that in the Kongo understanding there is only one real culprit: the one who started the fight. Any wrongdoing as a reaction to that one initial evil act is not seen as 'sin' and is thus not to be punished.

Nzambi, *the Far Away and Paradoxically Close God?*

God is the missing element when it comes to wrongdoing and evil in the Kongo culture. When I asked the students where *Nzambi* (God) would come into the picture of wrongdoing and 'sin', the answer was: '*He does not*'. The Kongo tradition views *Nzambi* as a God distant from human beings.

Humans do not deal with God and *Nzambi* does not object to their wrongdoing. The students were surprised how close God was to the people of Israel, and that Yhwh was offended by an act comitted by mortal beings. In Kongo belief, God does not intervene, it is the ancestors whom mortals are attached to, and the ancestors are attached to *Nzambi*. Together with the *banganga*, the ancestors take

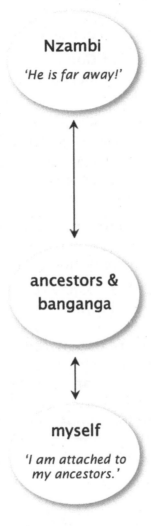

Hierarchy of human beings – ancestors – Nzambi

37

the place of 'intermediaries'. The students explained that traditionally *Nzambi* is far away, and that is why *Nzambi* is not offended or even touched by a bad action.

The Kongo understanding of God is still marked today by some confusion and theological misunderstandings. To my question of why there is so much confusion, a student answered:

> *The white man is curious. He seeks to know. Why this? Why that? Why? ... [But] when you look in the African culture, God is mystery. The African doesn't try too much to understand the mystery. He takes it as it is and he leaves himself to the mystery.*

The view of God being a mystery and the students' ambivalent understanding of *Nzambi* found wide echo in the literature. The findings in the literature are presented in the following.

The name *Nzambi* – *Nzambi a Mpungu Tulendo* in the traditional full name – is not unique to the Kongo culture. It exists in many variations and is used throughout the western part of the central African region to designate the Supreme Being. Yet the Kongo people did not use the term exclusively for the Supreme Being. *Nzambi* also designated a human being (alive or dead), the first whites, a spirit that could be invoked for rain, parents, a paramount chief, mysterious, unusual things or a huge animal.[22] The name *Nzambi* derives from the root *nza* (light) or *nzazi* (lightning).[23] It has been suggested that *Nzambi* was originally a royal title;[24] it was only through the Christian mission that the word

---

[22] Karl E. Laman, 1962. *The Kongo III*. Sweden. (Studia Ethnographica Upsaliensia; XII).

[23] Karl E. Laman, 2000. *Rayons de vérité - suivie de: Là où les ténèbres se dissipent.*

was established to mean exclusively God's name. *Mpungu* is commonly used for the Supreme Being, and it filled the role of a patron or protector of the village,[25] but the original meaning remains obscure.

Information about *Nzambi's* character turned out to be diverse and contradicting as well. In general, *Nzambi* is identified with creation, power and freedom.[26] He is everywhere, sees everything and knows everything.[27] Others described him as living in the sky and thus unable to visit the earth; he did not show himself to people.[28] The Kongo people feared *Nzambi*, who was not somebody to be trifled with. *Nzambi* is perceived as good and evil at the same time; he 'does what he thinks right' and is of 'great unshakable spirit'.[29] Because the people believed that *Nzambi* had let death come and that he provided them with *minkisi* (objects with concentrated supernatural powers), of all sorts and dealing with all kinds of evils,

---

[24] William Randles, 1968. *L'ancien royaume du Congo des origines à la fin du XIXe siècle*. Paris: Mouton & Co. (Civilisation et Sociétés; 14); Joseph Thiel, 1983. 'Zur Diachronie des Nzambi-Namens in Bantu-Afrika'. *Zeitschrift für Ethnologie*, 108 (1), pp. 105–31.

[25] Joseph van Wing, 1938. *Études bakongo II: religion et magie*. Bruxelles: Institut Royal Colonial Belge. (Mémoires, Collection in-8°; Tome IX, fascicule 1).

[26] Georges Balandier, 1968. *Daily Life in the Kingdom of the Kongo: From the Sixteenth to the Eighteenth Century*. Translated from French by Helen Weaver. Cleveland, OH: The World Publishing Company.

[27] Kilandamoko Mengi, 1981. 'L'évangélisation missionnaire protestante face à la culture kongo. L'enracinement de l'Évangile dans une culture'. Thèse doctorale (PhD). Faculté de théologie. Université de Laval.

[28] Karl E. Laman, 1962. *The Kongo III*. Sweden. (Studia Ethnographica Upsaliensia; XII).

[29] Karl E. Laman, 1936. *Dictionnaire ki-kongo - français*. Brussels, p. 821.

'the people's relationship with him has never been marked by confidence or intimacy'.[30]

There is little doubt that *Nzambi* and the biblical God are thought of as equivalent by the Kongo people but this does not rule out the misconceptions about Yhwh. The book of Genesis portrays a God who enters a relationship of integrity with the world and does so in such a way that both the world and God are affected by that interaction. This stands in contrast to findings described above about *Nzambi*.

Kongo Renderings for the Christian Term 'Sin'

In the Protestant and Catholic churches in Congo, the term *masumu* is applied whenever 'sin' is mentioned. The students explained that everything that had been conceived as 'bad action' traditionally was translated by the missionaries as *masumu*, influenced by the first Bible translation into Kikongo in the early 1900s by Karl Laman. With the arrival of the Christian missionary, the Kongo culture and Christianity were 'brewed' together.

The original meaning of the term *masumu* suggests that it derives from the Kikongo verb *sumuka*, designating the traditional concept of ritual pollution, or simply breaking a law, a prohibition, or any other activity disturbing the communal life in the *kanda*.

Other terms designating the idea of a fault or misconduct beside the general use of *masumu* are:

---

[30] Karl E. Laman, 1962. *The Kongo III*. Sweden. (Studia Ethnographica Upsaliensia; XII), p. 57

1. *Lufuma*, which designates 'fault'. The derivation *kifuma* means deformity.

2. *Nsoki*, which is the most adequate word for translating 'fault'.

3. *Nkombo*, which also means 'fault' originally. Today, *nkombo* designates a goat because traditionally, when a case was judged, the offender was sentenced to pay a goat to the offended. In case of an illness, a goat was sacrificed for the sick person to get healed. The real word for goat is *ntaba*.

As the following chapter will show, the Kongo term *masumu* is not a good fit for expressing the Old Testament notion of 'sin'. The term implies the understanding of 'sin' as defilement or the breaking of a taboo. The term needs to be filled with new meaning and complemented by other terms and, in this regard, more theological and linguistic research is needed which cannot be offered within the limitations of this study.

Exegesis of Scriptures –
The Old Testament Understanding of 'Sin'

The breaking of God's covenant by the people of God is foundational to Christian understanding of 'sin'. This basic understanding and other fundamental insights are explored below.

The Golden Calf – Exodus 32

The 'sin' committed in Exodus 32 is idolatry by the people of Israel. The text leaves it open as to what Aaron actually intended by doing so, but by declaring that kind of celebration in the name of Yhwh, Israel did not only break the first two commandments, they also violated the third commandment by grossly misusing the name of Yhwh. Yhwh tempers his fierce anger; he is moved with pity, yet he does not waive his judgement. The slaughter in the camp was not ordered by Yhwh, which at first led me to assume that it needs to be understood as resulting from Moses' own anger. The brutality of the Levites was incomprehensible to the students. They pointed out that in their understanding the Levites killing their own people was nothing short of treason: it was fratricide. Some students expressed a certain empathy for Moses' order by pointing out that, as the leader, Moses was dishonoured by his people and was thus authorized to impose sanctions for disrespecting norms and rules of a village, clan, or family, who deserve punishment depending on the gravity of the transgression. The New American Commentary suggests a more careful reading of the passage, pointing out that Moses' order to kill was not his angry reaction, but Yhwh's word. Moreover, the Levites going back and forth through the camp from one end to the other means carefully and systematically approaching everyone and finding out whether or not they intend to return to Yhwh, abandoning their idolatry. Only the ones who did not repent but stayed committed to idolatry were killed, even if they were relatives, friends or neighbours of the Levites.

From a Kongo culture perspective God's intervention is surprising and God's closeness to the people is astonishing. Yhwh announces to Moses his punishment. Moses pleads for the people. Yet God's response to Moses makes clear that Yhwh cannot overlook what Israel has done. Moses' plea either to forgive his people or to blot him out of Yhwh's book is not granted. Moses cannot atone by sacrificing himself for 'sin' he did not commit. No one except Yhwh alone can do what Moses wants to accomplish.

Exegetical insights in summary:

- Exodus 32 identifies idolatry as 'sin'. The transfer of divine authority from the living God to a dead golden idol has severe destructive consequences.

- 'Sin' is understood as breaking the covenant between Yhwh and his people of Israel, shattering their relationship.

- God's reaction to 'sin' is that of 'burning anger'. Although God is reported to be moved with pity (v.14), he does not waive his judgment; he does not overlook 'sin' as if nothing had happened.

- The 'sin' by the people cannot be atoned for by Moses, who is willing to sacrifice himself, but will affect generations to come.

- 'Sin' makes God withdraw his presence. The people's abysmal grief indicates the deadly consequences that will arise from God's absence.

- For describing 'sin' the Hebrew term *ḥāṭā'* is used. It is understood as destructive behaviour, and as turning aside from God's instructions. Moreover, 'sin' has to do with the human nature, being stiff-necked and bent on evil. 'Sin' is also associated with impurity ('running wild') and is understood as bringing harm and death to the community.

The following exegeses will show if the above findings are further supported and could be generalized for the Old Testament understanding of 'sin'.

Achan's Theft – Joshua 7

The chapter starts with stating the 'sin' committed that led to the defeat in Ai: the Israelites 'broke faith in regard to the devoted things in Jericho'. The use of the plural form stands out (lit.: 'they, the people of Israel, acted unfaithfully'). Although Israel's doing is immediately specified in terms of Achan's individual action, it is nonetheless noteworthy at this point because it implies important insights regarding the Old Testament view of communal and individual accountability.

The spoil of the battle in Jericho was declared 'sacred'. It must not be privately used but handed over to the sanctuary (Josh. 6:19, 24). Yet Achan took what belonged to Yhwh, which was referred to as 'breaking faith'. Israel's 'sin' lies foremost in transgressing God's covenant by taking into their possession what belonged to Yhwh. In v.15 the 'transgression of the covenant' is paralleled by 'doing an outrageous thing'. It is only in v.20 that Achan confesses the 'sin' as his doing; the previous verses refer to it as Israel's. The intertwining of personal and communal responsibility for committed 'sin' flashes up again at the occasion of the punishment of Achan that includes his sons and daughters (v.24f).

The 'sin' committed in Joshua 7 does not seem to be as hopelessly devastating as it was in Exodus 32 however. Here a big 'if' is declared. If the people will destroy the banned spoil in their midst, they will again experience God's presence. The Word Biblical Commentary puts it quite simply: Israel must choose between the presence of God and the presence of the 'sacred things' set apart for Yhwh.[31]

The radical consequence for Achan is his capital punishment. Yet Achan's 'sin' has far more consequences than the death penalty for himself. Achan's theft has made the camp of Israel greatly vulnerable: they are 'unable to stand before their enemies; they turn their backs to their enemies' (7:8, 12). To re-establish their position and the ability to stand before their enemies and conquer Ai, the taken devoted things must be destroyed.

Achan and his livestock are stoned to death immediately; his possessions and the stolen goods are burned. Whether the family suffered the same fate is uncertain because the plural form in v.25 could refer to Achan's livestock and possessions alone, but also to the 'sons and daughters'. Deuteronomy 24:16 prohibits the death

---

[31] Trent Butler, 1998. *Joshua*. Word Biblical Commentary (WBC). Dallas, TX: Word Incorporated. (Vol. 7), p. 85.

penalty for family members of a malefactor unless they were accomplices in the offence committed.

If Achan's family was stoned without having anything to do with the theft it would indeed be deeply shocking, as the students pointed out in unison. The Word Biblical Commentary suggests a more likely explanation is to be seen in the conception of holiness.

> The spoils of war are devoted to God and are holy. As such they must be given over to God. Their holiness contaminates man. If they are brought into the camp they contaminate the entire camp, so that it must be sanctified, made holy. Anyone who had come into contact with the goods was contaminated and had to be removed from the community to protect the community.

Holiness is also linked to the Old Testament understanding of the community. Because Israel rigorously removes the contaminating 'sin' from their midst, God turns from his burning anger. With the banned goods no longer in their possession, Yhwh can again move among them. The Word Biblical Commentary points out that 'only as a holy people can Israel have the holy God with her'.[32] Israel shall never forget the incident. In order to keep up the memory, the geographic site is named after Achan: the valley is called Achor – 'Trouble' – thereafter.

The most important things to learn from Joshua 7 regarding the Old Testament understanding of 'sin' are as follows:

---

[32] Trent Butler, 1998. *Joshua.* Word Biblical Commentary (WBC). Dallas, TX: Word Incorporated. (Vol. 7), p. 86.

- The text displays the intertwining of an individual's act and the community's accountability (Israel broke faith, not just Achan), which points towards the issue of the 'corporate nature of the individual' in Hebrew thought.

- Achan's 'sin' is understood as a transgression of the covenant to which God reacts with anger. Yhwh's presence is at stake.

- 'Sin' is understood as rendering the transgressor unholy, contaminating the whole community. Thus, the unholy must be radically removed so that God can again live among the people.

- The individual's 'sin' has consequences for the whole community and leaves Israel vulnerable to the enemies.

- Yhwh intervenes by withholding his blessing (thus the defeat at Ai) and by identifying the culprit.

- For describing 'sin' the Hebrew term ḥāṭāʾ is used. It is understood as rejecting or denying Yhwh and is paralleled with foolishness.

Parallels to the text in Exodus 32 can clearly be seen already, and now let us consider King David.

David's Adultery – 2 Samuel 11–12

The narrative in 2 Samuel 11–12:25 starts with the note that it happened during springtime, the time when kings usually go out to battle. This, however, David did not do; he remained at home.

In contrast to the King of Israel is Uriah, Bathsheba's husband, who dutifully serves in the military, abstaining from homely pleasures such as eating and drinking and lying with his wife, although he gets invited to do just that. David sees Bathsheba and sleeps with her and she becomes pregnant. Because David's scheme to make it look as if Uriah was the father is not successful, he orders Joab, his commander-in-chief, to arrange Uriah's death in the war against the Ammonites. Although David did not touch Uriah, he had engineered his death from a distance and was as guilty of murder as if he had killed his servant with his own sword.

What David did 'displeased the Lord', and God sends the prophet Nathan to confront David. The divine intervention surprised the students. More surprisingly to me, however, is David, who faces up to the fact that he is without excuse and deserves the verdict he has just passed on the rich man in Nathan's story: he deserves to die. David confesses his guilt openly before the prophet. From my perspective this is extraordinary. The king's confession was understood as a loss of face. Nathan was God's mouthpiece but still one of David's subjects. Nathan's response to David's confession sounds logical. 'The Lord has put away your sin; you shall not die.' God's forgiveness, however, cannot be taken for granted. The law declared that all murderers and adulterers must die (Ex. 21:12) yet Yhwh declares that that will not happen to David.

God's immediate forgiveness is also extraordinary because it was granted without requiring David first to make animal sacrifices or give gifts to Yhwh. It also points toward an important difference from the case of Saul who had 'rejected' God's word as well. David's confession and forgiveness are the clearest indication that in the most essential relationship of all – that of submission to Yhwh – David was different from Saul. David accepts his guilt and repents without looking for any excuse. In my view this incident in David's life shows why David was called 'a man after God's heart' (1 Sam. 13:14). Psalm 51 shows clearly that his repentance was not just lip service (as Saul's seemed to be in 1 Sam. 15:24f), but sincere regret and submission to Yhwh.

David's repentance, however, does not mean that the judgements which Yhwh has announced through Nathan have been annulled: the consequences for having 'utterly scorned the Lord' still need to be faced.

Nathan explains that the repercussions of his 'sin' will affect his family for years to come. The punishment that Yhwh meted out reflects the crimes committed. Bloodshed ('the sword') will never depart from David's house and Yhwh will raise up trouble against David from within his own family. As far as his wives are concerned, he will lose them to a companion, all Israel witnessing it. The continuing narrative will show that the consequences worked out during David's lifetime, bringing tragedy and loss to mark the later years of his reign: Amnon's violent death, ordered by his half-brother Absalom revenging his sister's rape by Amnon (2 Sam. 13); Absalom's rebellion and his appropriation of David's harem (2 Sam. 15:1–12); Absalom's murder by David's loyal commander-in-chief, Joab (2 Sam. 18); Adonijah's attempt at taking the throne (1 Kgs 1–2). 2 Samuel 12:15 attributes the sickness of David's child directly to Yhwh and thus associates the illness of the child with the 'sin' of his father David. The text itself says that the child has to die because David 'utterly scorned the Lord'. Forgiveness does not mean that Yhwh's judgement has been annulled; the consequences of the wrongdoing still have to be faced.

The story of David's adultery, a 'tale of alienation and judgment', does not end with the painful and deadly consequences of David's 'sin', however. A brief and stunning note of another son's birth is made (2 Sam. 12:24f). And this birth is marked by Yhwh's love, not judgement. What a gesture of God's grace.

The following insights on the Old Testament understanding of 'sin' emerge from the above:

- 'Sin' is identified with despising God's word, which means despising God himself.

- David's adultery and act of murder are clearly understood as being directed against God.

- Repentance and declaring the forgiveness of the 'sin' committed does not mean that the consequences are all annulled.

- 'Sin' affects the whole family immediately (in terms of sickness and death), but also over generations. Moreover, it leaves a mark on David's life.

- For describing 'sin' the Hebrew term *ḥāṭā'* is used again. It is understood as deeply disrespecting Yhwh and having evil, calamity and death in tow.

Closely linked to the text of 2 Samuel 11–12 is Psalm 51, whose author is probably David himself.

Psalm 51 – David's prayer for forgiveness and restoration

1. The psalm uses three different Hebrew terms for 'sin' – *pāša'* ('transgression'), *'āwōn* ('iniquity'), *ḥāṭā'* ('sin') – that seemed to be parallel. These terms are completed by further description of wrongdoing as being 'what is evil in God's eyes' (v.4).

2. The writer of the psalm experiences 'sin' as something from which he needs to be cleansed. 'Wash me, cleanse me, purge me', he asks God (vv.1, 2, 7, 9, 10).

3. 'Sin' is understood as being committed against Yhwh (v.4). Sin can be against oneself and against one's neighbour, 'but the flouting of God is always the length and breadth of it'.[33]

4. The description of the wrongdoer as being born a 'sinner' (v.5) seems to refer to the understanding that 'sin' is not only an act, but also a (human) condition that cannot be healed or mended by humans (v.6); only God is able to transform, to cleanse the heart and renew the spirit (vv.7, 10). God desiring truth in the 'inward being' and teaching wisdom in the 'secret heart' is like an alternative programme needed deep within the human being.

5. The reference made to hyssop in v.7 suggests that the 'sinner' cannot stay in God's presence and is excluded from the congregation (because of defilement). The law prescribed that the hyssop plant was to be used in purification rituals of lepers (Lev. 14) and of those who had touched a corpse (Num. 19:6, 18).

6. 'Sin' also affects the offender's emotions: joy and gladness are gone, having consequences for the person's wellbeing, (inner) strength and even health (v.8).

---

[33] Derek Kidner, 1973. *Psalms 1-72: An introduction and commentary on Books I and II of the Psalms*. TOTC. London: InterVarsity Press. (The Tyndale Old Testament Commentaries), p. 190.

Word Studies

The Old Testament Hebrew language offers a wide variety of terms for describing 'the breadth and depth of the failure of the people of God'.[34] The different words for 'sin' in the Old Testament are not to be separated and contrasted with each other with analytical sharpness, but together they build the whole of understanding; they are not to be seen as synonymous either, but as complementary.

Universality and seriousness of 'sin'

'Sin' is humanity's basic problem (Gen. 3); every inclination of the thoughts of the human heart is continually evil (Gen. 6:5). God made the human race upright, but they have sought out many schemes (Eccles. 7:29). Wrongdoing in the world does not come from some other place than human beings.

There is a twofold 'mystery' about the 'sin' of God's people. First, there is Israel turning away from Yhwh who had repeatedly demonstrated his power and provision. Instead, they turn to 'resource-less' (*hebel*) gods and become 'empty' (*hubal*) themselves (Jer. 2:5–8). Second, Israel did not only turn away from Yhwh, but they persisted in their faithlessness. Although the people of Judah have seen what happened to their kinsfolk in the north, they still refused to listen and to turn from their wickedness (Jer. 44:1–5).

What the Old Testament describes in terms of 'sin' is relevant beyond the Old Testament Hebrew culture and the people of Israel.

---

[34] John Goldingay, 2006. *Old Testament Theology*. Vol. 2: Israel's Faith. Downers Grove, IL, Milton Keynes: IVP Academic; Paternoster, p. 257.

The nature of 'sin'

The passages discussed above revealed that 'sin' is understood as damaging behaviour, as turning aside from God's word, as rejecting Yhwh himself, as bringing harm and death to the community. 'Sin' is associated with defilement; it has to do with the human nature and is paralleled with foolishness. However, the nature of 'sin' cannot be encapsulated in one expression or picture. The Old Testament presents a wide variety of images. The texts discussed above present three main terms.

The Old Testament uses three main terms for 'sin': *ḥāṭā'* – image of missing a target; *'āwōn* – image of deviation and crookedness; *pāšaʿ* – image of mutiny and rebellion.

1. The term *ḥāṭā'* renders various actions that range from idolatry (Ex. 32), stealing devoted things (Josh. 7), adultery and murder (2 Sam. 11–12), offences against one's own brother (Gen. 42:22), or causing Pharaoh's anger (Gen. 40:1), to the drinking of blood (1 Sam. 14:33f), social misdeeds (Micah 6–7), etc. The diversity of actions designated by *ḥāṭā'* suggests that the term is extendable to every possible offence. Used in a more everyday language, *ḥāṭā'* refers to shooting at a target and missing it. This suggests that, in a religious context, 'sin' implies falling short of Yhwh's expectations. Moreover, the verb *ḥāṭā'* means not only to commit 'sin', but also 'experience misfortune' or even 'punishment'; it refers to both the deed and its consequences; it means to 'sin', to be guilty, or to bring calamity (upon oneself).

2. The noun *'āwōn* is the most common Old Testament Hebrew rendering for 'sin'. Although the deriving verb *'āwâ* (to twist) is far less common, a few occurrences (e.g. Lam. 3:9) suggest

the meaning of deviation or going astray. 'Sin' in that sense means that Israel has deliberately diverged from the way (Jer. 3:21). More clearly expressing the meaning of straying or erring is *šāgag/šāgâ*. As sheep stray and planners err (Ezek. 34:6; Job 12:16), so do people in relation to God (e.g. Job 6:24; Ps. 119:67). 'Whereas *šegāgâ* can imply unintended deviation from the path of rightness (e.g. Josh. 20:3, 9), *āwōn* is more inclined to imply a deliberate choosing of the wrong way.'[35]

3. The prophet Isaiah (1:2) compares Israel with rebellious (*pāša*) children. Israel was a rebel (*pāša*) from birth (Isa. 48:8) and has a stubborn and rebellious heart (*sārar, mārâ*, Jer. 5:23). In a vision God describes Ezekiel's audience as a 'rebellious house' (*merî*, Ezek. 2:6; also 3:9, 26) characterized by a defiant refractoriness. In this image Yhwh is the head of the household whose members do not submit to his authority as expected. In a different image the verbs *mārad* and *pāša* are used to denote revolt against a king or mutiny against an emperor (e.g. Ezek. 17:15; 2 Kgs 1:1). The image of rebellion links with that of the covenant relationship between Yhwh and Israel. Because 'they have abandoned the covenant of the Lord their God and worshipped other gods and served them' (Jer. 22:9) they are 'like the underling nations of a big power who have conspired to rebel'. *pāša* is a serious matter that most definitely affects the relationship between Yhwh and his people and for this reason has been described as the most serious term for 'sin' in the Old Testament.[36]

---

[35] John Goldingay, 2006. *Old Testament Theology*. Vol. 2: Israel's Faith. Downers Grove, IL, Milton Keynes: IVP Academic; Paternoster, p. 259.

[36] Rolf Knierim, 1997. peša'. In: Ernst Jenni and Claus Westermann, eds. *Theological Lexicon of the Old Testament*. Peabody, MA: Hendrickson Publishers,

Another perspective of the nature of 'sin' is seen in the contrasting concepts of good and evil found throughout the Old Testament. The term *ra*ʿ (evil) plays an important role in Old Testament passages that have to do with 'sin' and is often used in juxtaposition with its antonym *ṭôḇ* (good). These two fundamentally different concepts are usually held together; one does not seem to be thought of without the other. Moreover, the Old Testament describes *ra*ʿ as leading to death, *ṭôḇ* as leading to life. 'See, I have set before you today life and prosperity [*ṭôḇ*], death and adversity [*ra*ʿ]' (Deut. 30:15). To love *ra*ʿ and to hate *ṭôḇ* is to 'sin' (Mic. 3:2); and to call *ra*ʿ *ṭôḇ* calls Yhwh into action (e.g. Isa. 5:20). These concepts form the basis of Old Testament ethics.

Another issue of understanding 'sin' is to interpret 'sin' in the Old Testament not as an isolated (bad) action but as something that creates a sphere that sticks to the wrongdoer, a sphere that influences the surroundings, individuals, family, community, even a whole people. This 'sin-sphere' makes humans inwardly 'sick' and affects them also physically. 'Sin' has fatal effect on the perpetrator and remains invisibly associated with the offender, being 'pregnant with disaster'.[37]

God's reaction to 'sin' and its consequences

In the passages studied above it became apparent that Yhwh's reaction to 'sin' is first that of anger and rejection and of bringing

---

1033-1037. Also: Ludwig Koehler et al., eds., 1999. *The Hebrew and Aramaic Lexicon of the Old Testament*. HALOT (Logos electronic ed.). Leiden: Brill.

[37] Kurt Koch, 1974-2006. chāṭāʾ. In: Johannes C. Botterweck, Helmer Ringgren and Heinz-Josef Fabry, eds. *Theological Dictionary of the Old Testament*. Grand Rapids, MI, Cambridge: Eerdmans, pp. 309–319.

trouble, and sometimes death, upon the transgressor. Yhwh's withdrawal is not the only result of 'sin'. Wrongdoing leaves its mark on the transgressor as well. Psalm 51 most explicitly describes 'sin' as defiling, touching the transgressor deep inside, taking away joy and gladness, making him depressed and sick instead.

The two most predominant metaphors to describe 'sin' are a weight or burden that rests upon the perpetrator's shoulder (Ps. 38:4) and defilement, but there are other terms such as 'corruption' (*ḥānēp*). Job 8:13 describes a 'corrupt' person as somebody who forgets God.

The 'sin' committed by Israel is also described as 'affecting' God: The idolatry and the bloodshed in Jerusalem disgust Yhwh (Ezek. 22:2). Different forms of idolatry and idols put in the sanctuary are abhorrent to Yhwh (Jer. 4:1; 7:30; 16:18; Ezek. 5:11). And the offerings to other gods have 'estranged' Jerusalem so that Yhwh is no longer at home there (Jer. 19:4f).

The Old Testament paints an image of 'sin' leading to disaster and death. Yet its understanding of 'sin' is not complete without God's willingness for restoration. This is witnessed extensively in the psalms, and the Old Testament prophets' gloomy announcements of Yhwh's horrifying judgement are confounded again and again by God's unshaken determination to save, to redeem, to heal and to restore. Indeed, the pinnacle of the New Testament, Christ's sacrificial death on the cross and his resurrection from the dead, is foreshadowed in the Old Testament in the ritual of atonement (*kāpar*) in Leviticus 16 during which the *'āwōn* of Israel was 'loaded' onto a living animal who then literally carried it away into the desert, destined to die.

At the same time as recognizing the individual's responsibility, the Old Testament still emphasizes the reality of communal accountability. The understanding that 'sin' has consequences not only for the individual perpetrator but also for his family (or even the whole of Israel) over generations is accentuated in the belief that Yhwh 'visits' the iniquities of the fathers upon the children (Ex. 20:5; 34:7). It demonstrates that the responsibility of the community and its individual members of the present is extended into the past and into the future. Yhwh's announcement in Exodus that he will 'punish' children for the iniquity of parents and his promise in Ezekiel 18:2 and Jeremiah 31:29 that nobody will die because of somebody else's evil reveal a tension. The communal responsibility runs parallel to the individual accountability; they are set alongside and against each other. As it is impossible for the individual to hide behind the responsibility of the community, so the community cannot shelter behind faithful individuals.

Similar to the Kongo view of the community and the individual, the Old Testament understanding is that personhood is shaped, nourished and sustained in community; Israel is understood as a community, not a collection of individual selves, perhaps in contrast to a more Western autonomy and individualism.

'Critical Response' and Implications

The Kongo group participants granted me a glimpse of the cultural challenges Kongo Christians face, and with them we developed a series of propositions to help in their theological understanding. The theology students discussed, verified and revised the propositions.

Evaluation of the Propositions #1–4: Community Issues and 'Sin'

The first four propositions are grouped together because they concern 'sin' in connection with the Kongo view of the community.

Proposition #1: *Anything that threatens or destroys the harmony of the family is a 'bad thing'.*

Because the students perceived the Old Testament as saying the same thing as their culture, their suggestion for proposition #1 was unanimous: it is to be retained.

Proposition #2: *Doing a 'bad thing' is never private but affects the whole family (the whole community).*

The students' suggestion is to retain because it is according to Scriptures.

Proposition #3: *When the harmony of the family is threatened, death, diseases and curses enter the community and protection is no longer assured.*

Retain, as some of the students suggested. The consequences of evil in King David's family life became only too obvious. On the one hand 'sin' leads to all kinds of evil things, discord, divisions and illnesses, but on the other hand God protects against these very things, a tension that is difficult to understand and to bear. Both statements are true: 'sin' affects others (family) who are not directly involved, but God has the power to protect against what is perceived as the consequences of 'sin', yet at times, God's protection does not seem to 'work' and illness strikes and makes the innocent suffer. The best biblical example for this is Job, but the Kongo tendency to find the very source of calamity at all costs, usually sought in an individual member of the *kanda* – there must be a culprit or witchcraft – turns out to be enormously problematic as well at this point, for the story of Job does not endorse that view. Moreover, from the Old Testament perspective the power of 'sin' can only be broken by God's divine intervention: his forgiveness and restoration.

Proposition #4: *In the Kongo traditional view evil is something that is not innate but something that comes from the outside. In order to avoid 'bad things' being committed, the people must be 'educated'.*

Most students agreed that it is necessary to 'educate' in order to avoid or at least diminish wrongdoing, as the traditional view insists.

The Old Testament understanding of 'sin' as an almost 'thing-like substance' is an aspect that supports the Kongo view that evil can be an outside matter. I can be greatly affected by somebody else's evil, by the evil done by a whole community of which I am a member, although I might not have participated in doing evil. I might suffer 'innocently', like Job. At the same time, however, the Old Testament sees humankind as deeply corrupted, a condition that cannot be corrected by 'education' but that can only be healed by God's forgiveness and transformation. Moreover, everybody is called to responsibility as an individual, not hiding behind the community. The element of 'education', however, is also not to be overlooked in the Old Testament. I understand Proverbs, Ecclesiastes, as well as extensive parts of the Pentateuch and prophets as texts intended to teach, instruct and 'educate' audience and readers. Thus, I suggest modifying proposition #4.

The implications of the above evaluation touch on three main issues.

Search for the Source of Evil Breaking the Harmony

The Kongo people are keen to find the original source of the evil being perpetrated. Somebody must be responsible for the broken harmony that opens the door for curses and all sorts of evil to enter the community. It is essential to find the leak, because in the end it is a matter of life or death. In the Kongo culture the individual cannot really hide, at least not when the responsible party is searched for; all solidarity ends when evil enters the *kanda.* That vital search often means mortal terror for the individual. Once one is (unjustly) accused of being at the source of the evil happening, there is no turning back; there is only a slim chance of being excused or getting impartial, fair judgement. The only way out of being accused is often simply to confess to being the culprit even if one is not aware of any wrongdoing.

Forgiveness, foreshadowed in the Old Testament and firmly established through Christ in the New Testament, seems to be no real option in a Christian *kanda*. Moreover, the ethnic animosities in the classroom, and the tensions, the lack of compassion and unwillingness to forgive among future church leaders, as in the introductory grassroots story, were shocking and saddening. And this raises serious questions for the Church in Congo to answer. I see an immediate need for the Church to address these issues at congregational level but also on a national scale, offering courageous and honest dialogue that aims at reconciliation.

Fear of kindoki *and practice of* nkisi

Assuming that what I found in the literature regarding *kindoki* and *nkisi* applies to the Kongo context as well, the belief in 'witchcraft', especially the fear of being attacked by *kindoki,* needs to be openly addressed in the Church. To simply ban the practice is no solution because it touches not only on ethical behaviour but on the social structure, safety of the community and even on economics.

The practice of and belief in *kindoki* produce an atmosphere of fear that is deeply rooted in the social structure. *Kindoki* makes the Kongo people behave ethically because of fear. I suspect that this fear is transported into the Christian faith, leaving its marks on what is supposed to be 'Christian behaviour'. My experience was that many Kongo Christians are still driven by the fear of getting 'punished' by calamity striking if one does not do what is preached on Sundays or what the Bible or the leading pastor commands. The main features of ethical behaviour that are perceived as 'Christian' look very similar to the Kongo traditional understanding of wrongdoing, yet the motivation to behave ethically is fundamentally different. While ethical conduct in the Kongo culture is driven by fear, Christian ethical conduct is meant to be motivated by love. The possibility of unconsciously being *ndoki* aggravates the Kongo people's fear of being accused.

It places a burden upon many to meet the family obligations even if they constitute severe intrusions into the household economy. Everybody looks at everybody else in the family with suspicion; trust is often a foreign word. The suspicion paralyzes honest, supporting relationships that foster trust and confidence. In the Christian communities the call to exercise love in terms of 1 Corinthians 13 is often only paid lip service because of fear.

Simply banning the belief and practices of *kindoki* and *nkisi* is short sighted and makes the practices go underground. I suspect that the 'sources of influence and power' are rarely understood by the cultural outsiders, the missionaries. The churches influenced by West-European culture banned the use of *nkisi*-powers without offering an alternative. Because practices of *nkisi* are more than religious habits or beliefs, however, it is not surprising that many Christians still call on traditional powers. These sources of influence and power are part of the Kongo social and political fabric that cannot be banned without developing an alternative reliable system that takes into consideration the Kongo daily fears and affairs of evil, the basic questions that drive the Kongo search for 'good life'. A meaningful theological teaching about 'sin' needs to comprehensively reflect on the issue of *kindoki* and *nkisi*, developing an alternative that builds up a trustworthy community.

In order to find such an alternative, any further research undertaken needs to consider Pentecostal responses to the challenges and problems described in this sub-section. Kalu claims that Pentecostals root their message of the gospel into the African map of the universe and thus its fruits serve more adequately the challenges and problems arising from indigenous worldviews than the earlier missionary fruits did. 'The major contribution of the Pentecostal movement is how it addresses the continued reality of the forces expressed in African cultural forms'.[38] Although I found Pentecostal churches in Africa generally display great hostility to African traditional religions, their theology functions within a worldview that deeply resonates with indigenous religiosity. Pentecostal churches may give a 'Christian answer' to the specific religious needs of the African soul that 'provide their followers with the weapons of the Spirit they need to fight back against the forces of evil as they manifest themselves in disease and discord'.[39] At the same time, however, by offering 'treatment' against 'witchcraft' – divine healing services and ceremonies of exorcism – the Pentecostal churches are in danger of reinforcing the very practices and beliefs they fight, as a UNICEF study points out. 'The more God's servants fight against witchcraft, the more they get involved in treating witches, and at the end of the day, the more they extend the resources of witchcraft.'[40]

---

[38] Ogbu Kalu, 2008. *African Pentecostalism: An Introduction.* Oxford, New York: Oxford University Press, p. 178.

[39] Harvey Cox, 1995. *Fire from Heaven: The Rise of Pentecostal Spirituality and the Reshaping of Religion in the Twenty-First Century.* Reading, MA: Addison-Wesley Pub., p. 247.

[40] Aleksandra Cimpric, 2010. *Children Accused of Witchcraft: An Anthropological*

Because 'witchcraft' is complex, its solution will be multidimensional, including the religious, political, social and personal dimensions.

Kongo Christian lifestyle and church model

Despite the problematic issues regarding the community described above, the community as the Kongo centre of 'good life' needs to be maintained. However, 'the missionary ideal of a Christian – individually saved, economically self-sufficient and socially autonomous – is the Kongo ideal of complete anarchy'.[41] Therefore, the Kongo ideal Christian life will look different.

To become a follower of Christ implies an ontological shift because of the following. One of Christ's most radical words regarding the life of a disciple is found in Luke 14:25: 'Whoever comes to me and does not hate father and mother, wife and children, brothers and sisters, yes, and even life itself, cannot be my disciple.' Considering the findings regarding the community, Jesus' call would mean for Kongo Christians to break with their ancestry, to leave their *kanda*, which amounts to losing 'life', security and prosperity; it would mean to die to their ontological selves, a call from life to death. It stands to reason that questions arise as to whether such an interpretation of Luke 14:25 is too radical or whether someone can become a member of God's family while still being tied into the former family, the former commitments, obligations, rights and privileges. I came to understand these issues as problematic.

Study of Contemporary Practices in Africa. UNICEF WCARO. Available at: <http://www.unicef.org/wcaro/wcaro_children-accused-of-witchcraft-in-Africa.pdf> [Accessed 20 June 2016], p. 3.

[41] Wyatt MacGaffey, 1970. *Custom and government in the Lower Congo.* Berkeley, Los Angeles, London: University of California Press, p. 254.

The courage to break one's cultural and familial ties and 'abandon the gods of his ancestors (Joshua 24:2) out of allegiance to a God of all families and all cultures' is what Volf describes as 'Abrahamic revolution'.[42] Abraham's call to 'go from his kindred and his father's house' (Gen. 12:1) meant to step out of 'enmeshment in the network of inherited cultural relations'. If 'becoming a stranger' and 'leaving one's family' is really what a follower of Christ must do, it would be of fundamental and existential importance that there is a new community into which the Kongo Christian would be 'born', new ties, new ancestry, a new line of blessing.

Some theologians have suggested developing a 'kingdom culture'. No Christian or church can exist free from a specific culture; Christianity, however, cannot be identified with that culture either. It must be asked what a 'kingdom culture' would look like as it takes shape in the local context. Whatever changes and transformation may be implied, the church of the local 'kingdom culture' is thought to be 'seasoned with grace, truth, and righteousness of the gospel of Jesus Christ' and 'will be a faithful sign, instrument, and foretaste' of Christ's kingdom.[43] The Kongo version of the 'kingdom culture' would take over the role of that new *kanda*, meet the needs of its individual members and address the problematic issues described in this study; it would take over the responsibilities, tasks and necessary roles of the Kongo community, allowing 'good life' to be lived.

---

[42] Miroslav Volf, 1996. *Exclusion and Embrace: A Theological Exploration of Identity, Otherness, and Reconciliation.* Nashville, TN: Abingdon Press, p. 39.

[43] Craig Ott, 2015. 'Globalization and contextualization: reframing the task of contextualization in the twenty-first century'. *Missiology: An International Review,* 43 (1), pp. 43-58, p. 52.

Evaluation of Propositions #5–6: Concerning God and His Involvement in Human Affairs

Proposition #5: *In the [Kongo] traditional view God is not affected by the 'bad things' committed by human beings because he is far away from the living.*

Although the majority of the students agreed that the traditional view contradicts the Old Testament view, two students suggested the proposition not to 'reject' but to 'transform':

> Mt. 28:20 *"I am with you always..."* So the cultural element is not consistent with the biblical thought. Hence, we stress the transformation of this element ... It is a mistake to believe that God is not affected, and that he lives far away from us. No! That's wrong. This element is to be rejected or modified.

That the transformation is not just to be made intellectually was suggested by yet another participant:

> [The] *fifth cultural element must be transformed in order to change the African's traditional mentality.*

The Kongo perspective of *Nzambi* being far away is still to be kept in view; God is both, the utterly other, unsusceptible to human manipulation, but also close, intimately relating to humankind. As one student expressed it, God is mystery indeed.

Proposition #6: *Contrary to the traditional cultures in Congo, the God of the Bible is truly touched by the sin of his people (or by the sin of an individual) because he is near, because he is committed to his people by a covenant.*

All students without exception agreed that this is to be retained:

> *The Bible does not talk about a distant God, hence the need to transform this cultural view that teaches that God is not affected by the sin of his people.*

Accepting proposition #6 also means that 'sin' is to be viewed as being committed 'before God', and not only 'before the community'. It would be worth reflecting further on the question whether the Old Testament does support the view of 'sin' being committed 'before the community' or whether it is exclusively understood as 'before God'. The Old Testament radically displays a God-centredness which seems to put the community at the periphery. This implies that the Kongo (Christian) people must understand that whoever does wrong is not only accountable to the family/community (*kanda*), but even more so to God.

The implications of the propositions #5–6 regarding the traditional Kongo understanding of *Nzambi* being distant, and thus wrongdoing not being 'sin' before God, are evident. The inquiries presented in chapter 4 showed that Yhwh takes centre stage in the Old Testament understanding of 'sin'; 'sin' cannot be thought of or discussed detached from the concept of God. This is not only true for the Kongo context, but also for my own culture. Whatever is thought about God influences the understanding of 'sin'. This implies that, if the Church is not able to comprehensively talk about God, the Church is unable to intelligibly talk about 'sin'. This applies for the Kongo context as well as anybody else's context.

God is deeply involved in human affairs, but not solely as a punitive God. From the beginning God is a blessing God, and his goal has been to give and sustain life. I am convinced that if the Kongo Christians firmly hold onto their image of God based solely on the view of the traditional *Nzambi* figure, ignoring or even refusing what is revealed about the covenant God in the Old Testament, they will not find the 'good life' they are yearning for. They will be like Israel, who abandoned the fountain of living water, digging out their own cisterns for themselves, cracked cisterns that cannot hold any water (Jer. 2:13). Understanding God in terms of the portrait given in the Old Testament is not an optional extra, but an essential part of the Christian life.

Evaluation of the Proposition #7: Discourse on 'Sin'

Proposition #7: *In the Church the terms 'bad things' or '(commit) evil' are generally translated by 'masumu'.*

I anticipated a vivid wish to modify and develop the Kongo vocabulary for 'sin'. I was disappointed. Many participants saw no necessity for change. It was, however, acknowledged that the Bible offers a much wider semantic field than the term *masumu* could possibly cover. Thus, one participant formulated the need for modification more resolutely:

> We note that several terms used in the French and Hebrew versions are generally summarized in our cultures by one single term. This can be explained by the poverty of our languages. In our opinion the concept of one single term referring to sin is to be rejected.

The perceived problem of the Kongo languages being too poor to express the concept of 'sin' more accurately was made most explicit in the following contribution:

'Translating "bad thing" or "doing evil" by masumu shows the emptiness of words that exists in the [our] culture ... We think that this phrase is neither to be kept, nor transformed, nor rejected, but it needs to be adapted corresponding to the [individual Hebrew] expressions.

The Kikongo version of Psalm 51 demonstrates that a variety of imagery for 'sin' can be accurately expressed in the Kongo language. Establishing a richer vocabulary and imagery than the word *masumu* portrays would most definitely help to understand the Old Testament concept of 'sin' more comprehensively.

Another way of developing a richer vocabulary and discourse of 'sin' could be contrasting terms, also analogous to the Hebrew sphere of 'sin'. Whenever we deal with 'sin' and offence – as offender or offended, as pastor, mediator, missionary, etc. – it is not only the one having committed 'sin' who must be addressed, but also the people who are influenced by the 'sin- sphere' and might greatly suffer the consequences.

Evaluation and Implications of the Contextualization Process and the Work across Cultures

While acknowledging that there was no 'single Kongo universe', I had assumed two distinct and relatively 'pure' cultures, the Kongo culture and my own Swiss culture. I thought of the issue being to communicate from one culture to the other, building a bicultural bridge and myself becoming a bicultural person who was able 'to see the world through the eyes of two cultures'[44] while being

---

[44] Paul G. Hiebert, 1991. 'Beyond anti-colonialism to globalism'. *Missiology*, 19 (3), pp. 263-82, p. 276.

aware of the Old Testament context being a third culture element to be considered.

The cultural context of the Kongo has been changing rapidly. The majority of the Congolese participate in different realities at the same time, and globalization, and with it hybridization, has dramatically increased the rate and depth of change. And if culture change is considered as something normal and neutral, there is no need to pit the 'traditional culture' or the 'past beliefs and customs' against outside influences. That leaves the uncomfortable question, however, as to whether and to what extent 'culture' is to be protected or preserved. With the cultural contexts being more and more hybridized, 'we are much better off as nomads between a plurality of cultures, than as self-imposed prisoners of a smug Euro-centrism (or Afrocentrism, for that matter)'. 'Culture' is no longer bounded, tied to a place, impossible to combine, blend and transgress.[45]

'For too long theology has been done by cultural outsiders.'[46] Although many authors writing about contextualization ascribe to the outsiders an important role because of their ability to see aspects of culture to which insiders may be blinded, the message that filtered through to me was simply 'you should not be doing what you are doing and how you are doing it': that is, contextualizing theology in a foreign culture. This increasingly brought into question even my

---

[45] Wim van Binsbergen, 2003. *Intercultural Encounters: African and Anthropological Lessons towards a Philosophy of Interculturality.* Münster: Lit Verlag, p. 521, p. 508.

[46] Ruth Julian, 2010. 'Ground level contextualization'. In: Matthew Cook et al., eds. *Local Theology for the Global Church: Principles for an Evangelical Approach to Contextualization.* Pasadena, California: William Carey Library, pp. 57-74, p. 68.

employment in Congo. However, I learnt that the challenge of doing theology cross-culturally is to be understood as having the creative potential for transforming participants as well as the contextualization initiator's perspectives. Doing theology cross-culturally moves and broadens one's (theological) horizon.

Contextualization is a complex undertaking. The discovery that community is central to understanding wrongdoing, however, unearths yet another point of special significance: it shows that 'sin' cannot be discussed as an isolated issue. The problem of 'sin' interrelates with the whole fabric of relations within the community and its sources of power: *kanda, kitaata, nganga* and *kindoki.* 'Sin' is not an isolated theological, anthropological, sociological or religious problem; all these areas are involved and even more areas (for example, peace-building and reconciliation, urban studies, globalization, etc.) could be taken into consideration as well, which makes the study of the topic of 'sin' very complex. My concept of community that is inclined towards autonomy and individualism is simply different from the ontological communal outlook of the Kongo people that makes it unthinkable for an independent individual to stay healthy or even alive.

The experiences in my research project demonstrate that it is not advisable for the process of contextualization to be done either by cultural outsiders or by cultural insiders alone. 'Western churches may acknowledge in theory that they have much to learn from Majority World brothers and sisters, but in practice a spirit of superiority generally prevails.'[47]

---

[47] Craig Ott, 2015. 'Globalization and contextualization: Reframing the task of contextualization in the twenty-first century'. *Missiology: An International Review,* 43 (1), pp. 43–58, p. 54.

Theological misunderstandings across cultures will most certainly remain, leading, however, not to the adverse effects of irreconcilable theological conflicts, but hopefully to the advantages of developing a deeper understanding. Recognizing and working through my misunderstanding of the importance of the Kongo community eventually led me to new insights that could be made fruitful for the Kongo context, but also for my own cultural context. In this sense, contextualization always works both ways.

Summary

As expected, the Kongo understanding of wrongdoing has similarities as well as differences to the Old Testament understanding of 'sin'. From my cultural outsider's perspective I conclude that the Kongo view of wrongdoing has surprisingly more to offer for the deeper understanding of 'sin' than I thought when I first started the research. The discovery about God not being involved in the Kongo traditional perception of wrongdoing – a view that Kongo Christians need to reject – was as startling as the insight that the Kongo communal outlook of the issue ties right into the Old Testament understanding of the community's accountability; 'sin' affects many more people (and even creation) than just the perpetrator. Brought into perspective with the Old Testament understanding of community, the Kongo view offers points for reflection that positively challenge the individualistic conception of 'sin' that is characteristic of my cultural background.

The given 'critical response' to the seven propositions and the implications thereof touch on complex issues and can be summarized as follows.

1. The experience of many Congolese is that the cultural/ traditional obligation for finding the original source of evil often leads to unjust accusations which block the way to sincere forgiveness and reconciliation.

2. Ethical conduct in the Kongo culture seems to be driven by fear while Christian ethical conduct is meant to be motivated by love. Suspicion of having *ndoki* in one's ranks paralyzes supporting relationships that foster trust. To simply condemn and ban *kindoki* and *nkisi* practices is no solution. Reflection is needed by closely looking at the social and political fabric underlying those practices in order to find alternatives.

3. Becoming a follower of Christ means an ontological shift, leaving one's family and being 'born' into another ancestry. Further reflecting on developing a local 'kingdom culture' is promising and a passable way for the Church to be transformed into a wholesome foretaste of Christ's coming kingdom.

4. God is deeply involved in human affairs, not only as a God of justice and righteousness, but as the one giving and sustaining life. Not understanding Yhwh (God) as a relational God leads to not understanding 'sin'.

5. A transformed view of 'sin' includes comprehending it not only as an isolated act, but also as generating a sphere surrounding the 'sinner', affecting him and others negatively. To understand 'sin' as a sphere, however, calls for further research. It also calls for the development of vocabulary that is able to express the understanding of a 'sin-sphere' accordingly.

The evaluation and implications of the contextualization process can be summarized as follows.

1. In order to conduct cultural research in a globalizing world it is necessary to adopt a model of culture that is able to deal with the 'trend to blend' (hybridization).

2. The task of contextualization remains a must. Both cultural insiders and outsiders are needed; both can learn from each other. Because of unexpected local situations, cultural givens and the complexities of the issues being inquired into, contextualization is a continued undertaking that requires a scrutinizing look at one's own assumptions and the willingness to let one's beliefs, assumptions and practices be changed and transformed.

Conclusions

Cultural Context

The Kongo culture understands 'wrongdoing' as anything that breaks the harmony of the community and consequently gives opportunity for evil to enter the community. In traditional understanding, 'wrongdoing' has nothing to do with God. The cultural key elements to be addressed for communicating the notion of 'sin' to the Kongo people are the community (or *kanda*), the issues of *kindoki* and *nkisi*, the understanding of evil being an outside as well as an inside matter (the corruption of the human heart), the image of *Nzambi*, and the Kongo vocabulary using *masumu* as the main term for 'sin'. Further research will have to address yet other issues such as forgiveness, restoration and reconciliation.

Three main difficulties of understanding for the cultural research outsider stand out.

1. The (mis)understanding of the Kongo *kanda* (or community) was a critical 'breakdown'. (This point is discussed in detail in

the original thesis.) In order to understand 'sin' in the Kongo context in more depth, that key element had to be included.

2. Another difficulty arose in terms of the Kongo society's hierarchical structure that did not allow me to freely choose my position; it was assigned to me. Coming to terms with my given authority position led me to revise my hidden assumption about the premise of the 'priesthood of all believers'. It also led to the revision of methods and of procedures for conducting the research. (This point is discussed in detail in the original thesis.)

3. Another unexpected issue was the traditional understanding of *Nzambi*. With the perception of *Nzambi* being distant, the notion of 'sin' can hardly be understood in terms of the biblical findings. Hence, inquiries into the image of God (in cultural and in biblical terms) needed to be included in the study.

Discourse on 'Sin'

The term 'sin' (Munukutuba/Kikongo *disumu*) is hardly used in the traditional Kongo vocabulary. The most frequent vernacular renderings for 'wrongdoing' (before missionary times) are all variations of the word (*yi*)*mbi* (evil, bad). Although the verb *sumuna* (from which *masumu* probably derives) comes up on lists of semantics used for 'sin', the origin of the term is unclear. The verb designates either 'uprooting a plant' or 'defiling oneself' by violating a taboo. For designating the different actions that are understood as (*yi*)*mbi*, a wide range of terms is used.

The term *disumu* (usually used in the plural form *masumu*) is mostly understood as the Christian religious term for 'sin'. It is not suitable, however, for rendering the diverse metaphors and meanings and the wide Hebrew semantic field of 'sin'. An alternative would be to adopt the imagery of the Old Testament and to develop a new, more comprehensive vocabulary.

The Old Testament notion of 'sin' is primarily understood as rebelling against Yhwh, breaking the covenant he made with his people. God takes centre stage; 'sin' is always committed 'before God' and is seen as directed against him. When 'sin' is committed, God actively intervenes. The Old Testament does not know one exclusive term for 'sin'; there is a wide variety. Three main terms stand out: *ḥāṭā'*, *'āwōn* and *pāša'*, each presenting a different image. The terms *ḥāṭā'* and *'āwōn* display an ambivalence in meaning ('sin', guilt and punishment) indicating that 'sin' and its consequences are not radically separate notions but could be understood as a 'process'. The Old Testament views 'sin' not just as an action but also as a power from which human beings cannot escape by their own efforts; it is deeply ingrained in the human heart. To 'sin' also means to endanger the community in so far as 'sin' has negative consequences affecting family and community as well as the individual transgressor. 'Sin' is connected to death and contrasts with the good or with life; it is often paralleled with evil and consists in the absence of what God is. 'Sin' has impacts on the transgressor, defiling him, weighing him down and taking away joy, strength and health. 'Sin' can only be forgiven, and the human heart only be transformed, by God's intervention.

The Old Testament view that the covenant God takes up a decisive and active intervening role when 'sin' is committed stands in stark contrast to the Kongo discourse. The Kongo people also regard differently the Old Testament perception that doing evil affects God; in the Kongo tradition, *Nzambi* is not involved in human daily affairs. The finding that 'sin' in the Old Testament puts the community in danger corresponds with the Kongo understanding of 'wrongdoing' letting evil enter the community. Another view in common is the understanding that 'sin' affects others (also physically), even generations. The deed-consequence or the cause and effect operating in human experience is found in the Old Testament but also in the Kongo culture: the Kongo people generally believe that calamity striking is a consequence of someone's evil deed. There is a difference, however. While in the Old Testament it is God who actively intervenes, in the Kongo tradition it is a mechanical, magic-like operation at work.

The 'critical response' given to the Kongo discourse in the light of the Old Testament understanding of 'sin' (in the contextualization model's terms of 'retain' – 'modify' – 'reject') can be summarized in seven main points:

1. The importance of the community in the Kongo culture is uncontested. The Kongo view that anything that threatens or destroys the harmony of the *kanda* (community) is a 'bad thing' is also to be 'retained'. The Old Testament understanding of community is, however, different from the *kanda* concept in the Kongo culture. Because it is Yhwh who takes centre stage in the Old Testament understanding of 'sin' and not the community (as it does in the Kongo culture), therefore further critical reflections on the *kanda* are needed in order to make it fruitful for the contextualization of 'sin'.

2. The Kongo view that 'wrongdoing' affects others is to be 'retained'. However, it needs to be complemented with the understanding that God is also 'affected' when it comes to 'sin'; to 'sin' means always to 'sin' against God who is the founder and sustainer of humanity and deeply involved in human affairs.

3. When the harmony of the community is destroyed, calamities and death enter. This view is to be 'retained'. Yet, the members of the community are not doomed to helplessly surrender to the cause-and-effect connection. God alone has the authority to break the power of 'sin'. The search for the responsible party for the breach is vital in the Kongo understanding. It often means, however, mortal terror for the (wrongly) accused. A design for forgiveness and reconciliation is hardly to be found in the Kongo culture, which runs counter to the Old Testament and New Testament. Similarly, the practice and firm belief in *kindoki* produces an atmosphere of fear; ethical behaviour is maintained because of fear being targeted by 'evil'. A trustworthy and supporting community cannot be built on such weak ground. The Christian faith calls us to exercise love in terms of 1 Corinthians 13. The Kongo obligation to find the source of evil in order to restore harmony and the practice of *kindoki* as a measure to keep the community members in line are to be strongly 'rejected'. Simply banning *kindoki*, however, is not the solution. Under the aspect of the community it is also important to point out that becoming a Christian might imply an ontological shift, leaving the old ancestry, which is radically counter-cultural. In order still to be able to live a 'good life', a community or Church model is required that can truly offer an alternative *kanda* that is tied into a new ancestry.

4. The Kongo traditional view that 'sin' and evil are not innate but come from the outside of the person needs 'modification'. On the one hand, evil does come from the outside and one can suffer by someone else's fault. On the other hand, 'bad actions' cannot be avoided by simply 'educating' the members of the community, because the corruption of the heart is also a fact.

The heart can only be healed by God, who alone is able to touch and transform the inmost being (Ps. 51).

5. In the Kongo tradition *Nzambi* is not affected by human 'wrongdoing'. This view is incompatible with the Old Testament understanding of God and is to be 'rejected'.

6. The Bible presents Yhwh as truly concerned by human 'sin'. Thus, in order to understand the concept of 'sin' and God's intervention and reaction thereto, the Kongo Christians need to embrace the understanding of God as the covenant God who is deeply involved in the daily affairs of their lives.

7. The common translation of 'sin' by *masumu* only – designating the breaking of a law – is too one-sided and thus inadequate and needs 'modification'. 'Sin' exclusively understood in juridical terms is misleading. No doubt, 'sin' has a morality component, but the view of the Old Testament is much wider than 'sin' being wrong behaviour breaking (moral) laws. In order to communicate the notion of 'sin' comprehensively, new vocabulary is to be developed, drawing from the imagery presented in the Old Testament.

Contextualization

The conclusions regarding contextualization and working across cultures can be summarized in four main points.

1. New models of contextualization are needed. In a globalizing world the view of cultures being distinct and relatively 'pure' that underlies many contextualization models is increasingly untenable.

2. The principle of the 'priesthood of all believers' has its cultural limits; it is not transferable to other cultures or to the work across cultures without reflection. It is not only the content of contextualization arising from the local context that needs adapting, but assumptions about the 'who' as well.

3. 'Sin' cannot be discussed as an isolated issue. The interplay between the Kongo understanding of 'wrongdoing', the community, *kindoki* and *nkisi* practices, with their social and political function, the image of *Nzambi* and missionaries' influence give a good example. Because of the complexity of the subject too narrow a focus is unsuitable.

4. The cultural outsider has an important role in the contextualization process. It is not advisable for contextualization to be done either by cultural outsiders or by cultural insiders alone. The process of learning from each other's understanding is vital.

Closing Thoughts

In the introduction I noted the suspected misunderstanding between the missionaries and the Kongo people regarding the understanding of 'sin' and conversion. I suggest that the misunderstanding had to do with the different narratives or questions asked by missionaries and by Kongo people respectively. From the findings of my research I claim that the misunderstanding still remains today. To caricature, many evangelical missionaries put emphasis on answering the supposed all-important question about how to get eternal life. The essential points of their answer are seemingly simple: in order to get eternal life, you need to get 'saved'. That answer, however, does not fit the question asked by the Kongo people because their question is different. They ask how they can live a prosperous and long life in harmony, protected from evil, in the here and now. From the perspective of the Kongo tradition, this question has nothing to do with God. In both narratives the problem of human 'sin' or 'wrongdoing' needs solving. In the missionary narrative God is involved because 'sin' – mainly understood as breaking a law given by God – is unrighteousness which breaks the covenant relationship with God. In the Kongo narrative God does not play any decisive role. The community is the central topic in terms of how it can be protected and how 'wrongdoing', understood as the gateway for evil that destroys life, can be avoided. Evil breaking into the community can be avoided by a) 'educating' the members of the community and b) taking different measures for protecting the community (e.g. *nganga* medicines, *kindoki* for protection). If despite all effort the harmony is broken and evil enters the community, it is essential to find out the origin and to correct the fault by sometimes drastic measures. Admittedly, the presentation of the two narratives is grossly simplified, yet it shows the discrepancy between the two more clearly.

Intriguingly, during my field work in Congo I noticed that in my home culture the questions asked today increasingly resonate with those of the Kongo people. In times of great uncertainty, unpredictable disaster striking, terrorism attacks, stock market crashes and the tides of refugees, the need for protection and security grows rapidly. That raises the serious question of whether the churches back home as well as the churches and missionaries in Congo are really fit to respond to the grassroots narrative, fears and questions. Surprisingly, I might find the results from this study conducted in faraway Africa most insightful for dealing with the fears and questions asked back home.

Having reached the end of my study, one thing keeps going around in my head. It is what John Calvin wrote at the very beginning of his Institutes:

> Nearly all the wisdom we possess, that is to say, true and sound wisdom, consists of two parts: the knowledge of God and of ourselves.[48]

If we want to live 'good lives' – a desire which I assume can be generalized for all human beings irrespective of culture – we need to know God, the founder and sustainer of life, as well as human beings with their proneness to forsake God, the fountain of living water, digging out cisterns for themselves that cannot hold water (Jer. 2:13).

Still emotionally marked by the March explosions in Brazzaville I left Congo in summer 2012 in a rather desperate mood thinking that 'good life' in harmony is not possible in Congo when even the Christians leave the fountain of living water not being ready to tread the difficult way of reconciliation. Remembering one student's tears and trembling, and the gripping atmosphere in the classroom during my preaching, my hope is sparked again. 'Sin' and its consequences can be healed and its powerful grip broken – God's restoration is also offered to the Kongo people and to Congo as a whole nation.

---

[48] Institutes, Book I, chapter 1, §1.

Glossary of Vernacular Terms

The Glossary presents only the most important terms used in the thesis. Additional terms as well as further explanations about meaning and usage are given in the text.

bakulu	ancestors (the dead persons of whom one still remembers the names)
bandoki	pl. of *ndoki*
banganga	pl. of *nganga*
bantima	pl. of *ntima*
buzitu	respect
dikanda	family / community
disumu	'sin'
kifuma	fault, deformity
kindoki	traditional power, 'witchcraft'
kintwadi	togetherness, being united
lufuma	see *kifuma*
luzingu	life
luzolo	
nsalasani	mutual love, support

masumu	pl. of *disumu*
mbi	bad, evil
mbongi	traditional institution for meetings of the elders
mbote	good
mfumu	chief
minkisi	pl. of *nkisi*
ndoki	specialist exercising *kindoki*
nganga	traditional (herbal) doctor, healer
ngunza	'prophet'
nkisi	objects with concentrated supernatural powers, 'fetish'
nkombo	fault, goat
nsoki	fault, iniquity
ntima	heart
Nzambi	God
nzambi	human being or kind of *nkisi*
yimbi	bad, evil